Communication Skills

Effective Editing

BOOKS IN ENGLISH LANGUAGE LEARNING SERIES

Grammar Matters

Common Errors in English
Dictionary for Misspellers
Idioms
Quotations
Proverbs
Riddles
Tongue Twisters

The Complete Guide to

Business Letters
Effective English Writing
Essays for Competative Examinations
Functional Writing in English
Modern Essays
Paragraph to Essay Writing
Prose Compositions
Résumé Writing
Letters for Social Interaction

Enrich Your Grammar

Antonyms
Current Words and Phrases
Prepositions
Synonyms
Word Perfect
Word Power
Word to Paragraph
Words and Their Usages
Word Origins

Communication Skills

The Power of Spoken English (with 2 audio CDs)
Speaking and Writing in English
Dynamic Reading Skills
Effective Communication
English Conversation Practice
How to Develop Profitable Listening Skills
How to Increase Your Reading Speed
How to Listen Better
How to Read Effectively and Efficiently
How to Resolve Conflicts

Communication Skills

Effective Editing

A practical handbook to develop good editing skills

Y. C. Halan

Sterling Paperbacks

STERLING PAPERBACKS
An imprint of
Sterling Publishers (P) Ltd.
A-59, Okhla Industrial Area, Phase-II,
New Delhi-110020.
Tel: 26387070, 26386209; Fax: 91-11-26383788
E-mail: mail@sterlingpublishers.com
ghai@nde.vsnl.net.in
www.sterlingpublishers.com

Effective Editing
© 2009, Y. C. Halan
ISBN 978 81 207 4763 0

All rights are reserved.
No part of this publication may be reproduced, stored in a retrieval system or transmitted, in any form or by any means, mechanical, photocopying, recording or otherwise, without prior written permission of the original publisher.

Printed in India

Printed and Published by Sterling Publishers Pvt. Ltd.,
New Delhi-110 020.

The book is

Dedicated to

The profession of journalism

and

Those who join it with high ambition

Acknowledgements

This book *Effective Editing* is based on my experience as an editor in four newspaper houses: Times of India, Indian Express, Hindustan Times and Observer. When I joined the Times of India Group in 1981 as the Editor of the *Career & Competition Times,* I did not know the ABC's of journalism, not to talk of editing and the responsibilities of an Editor. My colleagues in Times House took great pains to teach me the basics of journalism. It was at that point I thought of writing a book on editing. I came across great many things at the other three newspaper houses also. I am indebted to all the four newspaper houses for giving me an opportunity and a wide field to learn firsthand the various aspects of journalism that are replicated in the book.

During the last 28 years, I have interacted with hundreds of journalists in India and abroad and have picked up a little bit from every one. I am deeply grateful to all those numerous friends and colleagues who, knowingly or unknowingly, provided me inputs that became useful in writing this book. In particular, I wish to express my genuine appreciation to Alok Mehta, Editor-in-Chief of *Nai Dunia* and K. S. Sachidananda Murthy, Resident Editor of *The Week* for their encouragement and advice.

Sunny Thomas, my colleague in the Times of India Group, gave me capable and essential assistance by going through a few chapters.

Gopi Gajwani, an eminent designer, who also worked with me for almost a decade, carefully read the chapter on layout and suggested a few improvements. I am indebted to him.

Ajanta Dutt, Reader of English at Deshbandhu College, University of Delhi scrutinised the chapter on English language. I sincerely thank her for the assistance.

Special thanks to my daughter Monika Halan, for reading and rereading every chapter, providing clarity and conciseness to the book, and for being so responsive to my endless requests to read again and again.

As always Sonu, Jagmohan, Gautam, Karan and Meera have been a source of inspiration.

I am indebted to S. K. Ghai, Managing Director of Sterling Publishers who urged me to complete the book. It was his perseverance that forced me to finish the work.

Finally my wife Mridula for her unfailing support and enduring the bouts of excessive self-preoccupation that occasionally afflicted me during the course of my writing.

Preface

All editors, from sub-editors to Editor-in-chief, have to find a common ground between two conflicting goals—journalism and publishing. Journalism aims to provide information, enlightenment and entertainment to its large readership without cost considerations and constraints. Publishing, on the contrary, aims to generate profits by designing a newspaper or magazine that can attract moneyed advertisers. Every successful editor with the help of his team of journalists navigates between the two and makes the product work.

The purpose of this book is to describe the job and list those skills, for all those who are in the profession or are thinking of joining the profession or have just entered the profession with high ambitions. Practicing journalists aiming to move upwards may also benefit from having a point of reference and a source of ideas.

The art of editing falls into two categories: Journalistic skills that get you a job and the editing skills that make the unreadable readable. In the past, most of us learnt it through a painful process of trial and error. We do not want the newcomers to suffer from that pain and therefore this book. The book makes an attempt to cover the journalistic skills from the new perspective of editing.

No one has ever learnt editing from a textbook. No book can replace experience. But a book can offer a modest amount of encouragement and even inspiration, as well as be a source of relevant background information. It will help you to perform your job better equipped and ensure that you commit fewer nasty mistakes. You would learn the art and science of editing and would not find the language of your colleagues in the editing team alien. You will understand the way things have been done in the past. But none of this should stop you from doing what every journalist has to do—remake the job in the way that best suits your own abilities.

Always remember one uncompromising fundamental principle of editing—understand the reader and his interests. Good luck.

Y. C. Halan

Contents

	Acknowledgements	vii
	Preface	ix
1.	The Basics	1
2.	Editing: The Core of Journalism	12
3.	Editing Prerequisites	31
4.	Selecting News	58
5.	Editing the Main Story	76
6.	Heading or Headline Writing	107
7.	Writing the Introduction	128
8.	Understanding Language	153
9.	Layout and Design	173
	Glossary	193

1

The Basics

Background

Four fundamental inventions—fire, wheel, vote and language—have changed the course of civilisation. Language, in fact, has been the most powerful one as it has enabled mankind to effectively communicate with each other, locally in the beginning and globally now. The ability to communicate, in fact, is the most precious gift that God could have given to mankind. This was, probably, the only factor that enabled the society to move further and faster as time passed on. It was mainly responsible for the movement of civilisation from the most primitive stage to the most advanced one. No doubt human beings have been constantly struggling, since the beginning of civilisation, for the improvement, development and extension of God's greatest gift.

Communication has made human life dynamic, vibrant and vivacious. The International Commission for the Study of Communication Problems in its report *Voices One World* rightly calls communication, as the motor and expression of social activity and civilisation because "it leads people and peoples from instinct to inspiration, through variegated processes and systems of enquiry, command and control; it creates a poll of ideas, strengthens the feeling of togetherness through exchange messages and translates thought into action, reflecting every emotion and need from the humblest tasks of human survival to supreme manifestations of creativity—or destruction." It was communication that made the integration of knowledge, society and state possible, which in turn made communication more and more intricate and sophisticated.

Origin of Communication

Mankind owes its advancement entirely to communication. Having realised this, societies are constantly improving, extending and developing their abilities and capabilities to communicate with each other. No doubt, throughout history human beings have been trying to increase the impact, diversity and intelligibility of their messages. The first effort was to improve its ability to receive and assimilate information about their surroundings. Later it tried to increase the speed, clarity and variety of its methods of transmitting information.

The need for communication was recognised with the need to send warnings about hazards and threats and also to share the different ways in which these threats could be encountered. Initially the signals were simple. They were vocal and gestural. The most primitive societies developed a whole range of simple non-verbal means of conveying messages. These were: beating drums, lighting fires and making drawings and other graphic symbols on stones. With the development of language, communication became even more powerful.

Besides providing a range and depth to communication, language also gave precision and details to expressions. It simplified communication for individuals who were organising themselves into different types of societies that required interpersonal ways of exchanging information. As societies progressed language was widely used in education, science and technology, commerce, administration and law, and later research.

With the advancement of civilisations, different languages developed in various geographical locations. This was natural because there was no contact among people of different regions. People were scattered all over and were disconnected. They lived in small hamlets and villages and spoke a language that they had developed locally to communicate among themselves. So each habitation, even at a short distance from the other, would speak an entirely different language.

As people moved out of their villages and interacted with people from other areas, languages changed in response to new situations. The change was never-ending, at times gradual but most times rapid. Responses to new requirements and situations brought changes in the language. Emergence of new thoughts and knowledge, transformations in production techniques, and changing social, political and economic relationships made languages more sophisticated and rich. Language became essential to human progress. That is why different languages show some similarities as they all aim to take the human race forward.

After the development of oral communication, the use of script or writing that gave permanence to the spoken word was the next significant development in the area of communication. In the beginning around 6,000 B.C during the ancient Chaldaean civilization, writings were inscribed on baked-clay tablets. Then in around 2,000 B.C, scrolls of papyrus were used by Egyptians and later parchment was used that made binding possible. Books were handwritten in the Roman era. The Chinese were pioneers in the production of books. About two thousand years back, the Chinese emperors encouraged recording all the knowledge then available, particularly scientific and historical in a series of books. This probably was the beginning of the concept of history and an encyclopedia.

Communication in Ancient Times

The vast majority of people on this earth, for hundreds and thousands of years, lived in isolated areas. Confined to their own settlements, they were not in contact with other communities and the result was the creation of tribal areas or rural communities. Lack of mobility beyond their own living area forced them to communicate only among themselves.

Every village was an autarky. One living area was oblivious of the other even though situated only a few kilometers away. Life was slow, leisurely and more or less a routine because communication was among the same people day in and day out. As the inflow of information was almost zero, the interactions were dull, boring and caused frequent arguments and disagreements which led to clashes. However, life changed when someone came from outside the village. It was, however, a rare occurrence when some travelling stranger stopped by to stay for a night and told people about other far off places and what was happening there. Every word of the stranger sounded interesting. All listened to him spellbound because it was new to all of them (this became known as news). It briefly interrupted the boring routine of their diconnected existence and people waited for the next traveller.

Thus, it was an occasional spark in the routine and dull life of a community when travellers, pilgrims, nomads and soldiers visited them and narrated what was happening in other parts of the world. It changed the laziness and boredom of the community. As time passed and transportation became easier, visits by outsiders became more frequent. It fastened communication and brought people closer. It was unique as it gave new dimensions to communication and the human relationships.

With the passage of time communication became more intensive and faster. The movement of bards, scribes, traveling merchants, writers, voyagers and explorers across countries made communication wider. Interaction with them expanded the perspective and horizon of the people. Many of them recorded the happenings and transmitted these to the progeny. For example, Fi Hien came to India from China in the fifth century to study in detail the life and habits of the people in India so that China could understand them. Fi Hien was followed by Hsuan-Tsang in the seventh century during the reign of Harshvardhan when the T'ang dynasty was flourishing in China. He travelled through the Gobi Desert, Turfan, Kutch, Taskhand, Samarkand, Khotan and Yarkand, and entered India by crossing the Himalayas. He returned the same way he came.

He not only enriched the people who communicated with him during his travels but helped in establishing contacts between the governments of these countries. This was the beginning of the shrinking of the world; and its inhabitants grew nearer to each other. Common ideas began to spread which produced some measure of uniformity all over the world. On the political side, it led to the growth of democratic ideas.

However, till even two hundred years back, the news that reached the people was limited because it reached months after actual happenings. The human voice reached only those within its range, and the written message travelled no faster than a runner, a horse, a bird or a sailing ship. Despite these constraints, knowledge and ideas travelled great distances from their points of origin. The monks, priests and leaders of various religions carried the teachings of Buddha, Christ and Mohammed to the farthest corners of the world at a time when travel was slow, strenuous and hazardous. Nevertheless, the slowness of communication was responsible for the slow pace of change in societies, both within the societies and from one to another.

Despite all the limitations—slow, unreliable and disorganised—, news remained a significant aspect of every organised society. It covered many spheres of social life. In fact, all the developments in administration, trade, education, economic and military could not have been possible without the dissemination of news. But the societies remained passive and fatalistic making the ruler all-powerful. Transmission of news became more significant as societies became complex and economies developed faster.

The Modern Era of Communication

The invention of paper and printing was the forebear of the modern age of communication that caused spreading and proliferating knowledge and ideas through books. Development of mass information in the form of newspapers came later.

Books first appeared in China, India, and the Greco-Roman civilization and soon became the repositories of thought and knowledge. These were the best means of collecting a generous reservoir of information in a small space and in durable form. The invention of paper was the first significant advancement in the production of books. It replaced the old materials used for this purpose—papyrus or parchment. Paper was first used in China in the first century. It reached the Arab world eight centuries later and Europe could use it only in the 14th century.

The next great invention in the sphere of knowledge and communication was the technique of printing. China invented it in the ninth century. In 968, Wang Chieh published a book that was printed from blocks. It is supposed to be 'man's oldest printed book.' Another landmark was movable types used by another Chinese, Pi Cheng in 1045. Europe could use the printing technique only after six centuries, in the middle of the 15th century when Johannes Gutenberg of Germany set up one of the earliest movable cast metal type printing facility in Mainz. It was an important landmark in the history of newspapers. Gutenberg is acclaimed as the patriarch of the periodical press because, as S. H. Steinberg writes in *Five Hundred Years of Printing*, "When Gutenberg made it feasible to put on the market a large number of identical copies at any given time, he thereby foreshadowed the possibility of ever increasing the number of copies and ever reducing the length of time needed for their issue." He has been ranked as number one in *1000 years, 1000 People: Ranking the Men and Women Who Shaped the Millennium*, even before Mahatama Gandhi and Christopher Columbus.

William Caxton of Kent set up the first printing press in England in 1475. Nevertheless, no newspaper could be published in that country in the following two hundred years. The printing technique made it possible to produce several copies of the same book without much money and effort. This was a great step forward as it made the spread of knowledge easier, thus enabling the masses to get educated and enlightened. This, in a way, opened the road to liberalisation and empowerment of the common man—the *aam admi*. Consequently the literacy rate too increased at faster and faster rates.

The advent of printing press gave freedom of thought and expression to the people. Earlier kings and emperors did not allow disagreement. Nonconformist Hebrew scholars ran away with their manuscripts and went into hiding in caves. Socrates, one of the wisest men in history, was accused of corrupting the youth of Athens and had to drink poison in 399 B.C.

When introduced, the printing presses were not liked by those in authority. In fact, every technological advancement and new knowledge was often seen as a threat to the ruling power. Printing presses were not allowed to function and when permitted a licence was required that was not easy to procure. There were instances when printing presses were actually destroyed by the kings. Many scholars and scientists, who are now respected for their knowledge, wisdom and new thinking, were not allowed to publish their works. They were dismissed from universities and ordered to renounce their ideas under threat of dire penalties and imprisonment. Some were even put to death. But the bravehearts defied all prohibitions and threats and established printing presses. They printed books in large numbers, making authorities helpless as their diktats were not obeyed by the people. Renaissance and Reformation were possible only because of printing presses and the publication of books.

Printing, therefore, has broadened and liberalised the outlook of masses, empowering it with the strength to change even dictatorial governments under most oppressive conditions. The French and the Soviet revolutions are the appropriate examples. Nowadays the atlas has shrunk and is known as 'the global village.' The new means of communication—the Internet and mobile particularly, have empowered the people and have brought widespread transformation in societies across the world.

Origin of Newspapers

The earliest known newspaper was the Roman *Acta diurna* (Daily Events) and was established by Julius Caesar. It was produced on handmade paper. The first regular European newspaper after the invention of the printing press was *Avisa Relation order Zeitung* in Germany in 1609. In seventeenth century England, much before the newspapers were published, newsletters and pamphlets began to circulate. England's first daily newspaper was the *Daily Courant* in 1702. It was published by E. Mallet but he could not sustain it for long. Samuel Buckley restarted the paper and it became a remarkable newspaper in the following years. The *London Times* hit the stands in 1785 and the *Manchester Guardian* in 1821. The first American newspaper *Public Occurrence* appeared in Boston in 1609, but was soon suppressed. It was followed by the *Boston News-Letter* in 1704, the *Gazette* in 1719, and the *New England Courant* and *American Weekly Mercury* in 1721. The first daily newspaper in America was *Pennsylvania Evening Post* in 1783 but it could not last for more than 17 months. A new era in the American newspaper industry began in 1833 with the publication of *Sun* from New York. Priced at one cent, it was the first newspaper of the common man. It had a circulation of 8,000 as it carried human interest stories. An important landmark in the history of newspapers is 1851, as on 18th September the *New York Times*, priced at one cent, appeared on the news stands.

The first newspaper in India was the *Bengal Gazette* alias *Calcutta General Advertiser*, from Calcutta (now Kolkata) that came out in 1780. The *Indian Gazette* also began the same year. Madras (now Chennai) saw its first newspaper, *Madras Courier*, in 1785. Bombay (now Mumbai) had to wait till 1789 when the *Bombay Herald* was established. These papers were started by the British and were known as Anglo-Indian papers. These were either supported or opposed by the East India Company. The first real newspaper in India, *Calcutta Chronicle*, began from Calcutta in 1818. National newspapers were started later. *Statesman* started from Calcutta in 1875, *Times of India* from Bombay in 1838, and *Pioneer* from Allahabad in1860.

The significant point to note is that even in those days when there was a state of political conflict—specially a challenge to the established orders—the newspapers, more often than not, supported the popular cause. Tom Paine's *Common Cause*, for example, gave moral sustenance to the revolt of the American colonies against the British rule. The Indian press also, except the Anglo-Indian press, adopted an anti-British attitude and supported the freedom movement. In Latin America, similarly, the content and responsibility of a part of the press were connected with the struggle against Spanish domination that lead to their independence. The historians can find this link even today, both in the content of reporting and the way editors conceive their social and political responsibilities in this part of the world.

Today the newspaper, besides the electronic media, has become an indispensable tool of communication. It, in fact, is the major expression of social, political, cultural and business activity and is central to all social communication. In fact, the newspapers published in a country indicate the level of development and civility in that society. The reason is that newspapers express how the people think and behave and the way the society and economy is organised. They also translate thoughts into actions, reflecting every emotion and need from the humblest tasks of human survival to supreme manifestations of creativity. Therefore, as the society develops and moves forward the obligation of newspapers become more complex and subtle.

Newspapers have come a long way since their inception. Today the influence of newspapers is intermingled with changing social progress and structures. The effective mass media has brought to an end the long centuries of mass sufferings. India is an apt example, where the increasing influence of media is responsible for changing social processes and structures. The majority of the population now cannot be excluded from political life by sheer ignorance. People in the densely packed industrial towns and even in villages have became better informed than ever before and form their opinions on issues of controversy like the nuclear agreement with the United States. Public opinion has become a growing reality that no government can ignore.

The press—the Fourth Estate, as it is called—has established itself as an integral part of the modern constitutional state. Governments normally change as a result of elections and not simply through maneuvers within elite or at the whim of a monarch, except some countries in Asia and Africa. Whatever has happened in India during the past 60 years and is happening in the contemporary society is the best testimony of it. Nepal also testifies it, where in the early part of 2008 the monarchy was replaced by a republic after a successfully conducted election. It is an indication of the powerful influence of media in a society that is extremely poor and widely illiterate.

Today, the vast majority of people in many countries of the world are actively participating in the political life. In the United States it was due to the influence of the media that the largest number of voters (the percentage of 61 is the highest in American history) on 20 November 2008, came out of their homes to vote a black American, whose father was a Muslim, to become their 44th President. In India, because of newspapers, particularly the non-English ones, the masses are better informed and are forming their own opinion on controversial, social and political issues. The press has become a powerful organ of the society. It has established itself as an integral part of the polity, in which governments are changing because of people's participation in political decision-making. Also, newspapers are now strong enough to defy pressure from the authority. The way the Indian media has been successfully fighting governments (states and Union) to curtail its freedom of expression is laudable. The example of Pakistan can also be given where the military dictator, Pervez Musharaff was forced under media pressure to hold elections and hand over power to a popularly elected government in 2008.

In contemporary society it is an accepted doctrine that the press has a right and indeed a duty, to maintain its independence. This doctrine was formulated by John Delane, editor of *The Times*, in 1852. He had said, "We cannot admit that a newspaper's purpose is to share the labours of statesmanship or that it is bound by the same limitations, the same duties and the same liabilities as the Ministers of the Crown. The purpose and duties of the two powers are constantly separate, generally independent, sometimes diametrically opposite. The dignity and freedom of the press are trammelled from the moment that it accepts an ancillary position. To perform its duties with entire independence, and consequently to the utmost public advantage, the press can enter into no close or binding alliances with the statesmen of the day."

2

Editing: The Core of Journalism

A newspaper is the end result of several processes like planning the edition, allocation of stories and features, selection of edits and their writing, editing of to-be-published material, layout of pages and finally the production. The process is completed when the paper is delivered to the reader in the morning or afternoon. Of all the processes, editing is the most significant and plays a pivotal role in determining the quality of a newspaper.

Editing is carried out by the news desk which consists of a news editor, chief sub-editors and sub-editors;for convenience sake we will label all of them as desk-editors. In the contemporary media setup, copy editing is becoming another important aspect of editing. The process of editing begins when the copy of the story is filed by the reporter or the correspondent and is sent to the news desk. The process is completed when all errors are corrected and the story is made readable according to the style sheet of the newspaper. It is then sent for page layout. The final draft of the story is the workmanship and hard work of the desk-editor. The quality of editing determines the difference between a highly readable or even exciting story and a mediocre one.

WHAT THEN DETERMINES THE QUALITY OF EDITING?
We can say ten golden rules.

WHAT ARE THOSE RULES?
Let's examine them one by one.

The Ten Golden Rules of Editing

One—*Keep the reader in mind*: A newspaper is produced only for the readers; therefore, they are the the deciding factor and the final determinant of the quality of editing. If the readers do not like the newspaper they stop subscribing to it. The circulation falls and the newspaper may have to close down. *National Herald, Patriot, Observer of Business and Politics* and *Motherland* were newspapers which were closed down because of falling circulation. The *Hindustan Times* from Delhi and the *Times of India* from Mumbai had to discontinue their evening news tabloids. Since the readers are the buyers, they are supreme and their interests and requirements have to be kept in mind always. Therefore, while working on a story the guiding principle has to be—*how will the readers like it?* So the first rule is: the copy should always be edited from the readers' perspective.

Two—*Step into the shoes of the readers*: The desk editor should always presume that he is the reader and is reading the story in the newspaper. Therefore, one question should always be present in his mind—would I be interested in reading this story in the morning newspaper if it was not edited? And the other question would be—will I enjoy reading the unedited story? If these two questions were kept in mind, the desk editor will always come out with an excellent copy.

Three—*Try to use simple language*: Write simply. That means compose short and sharp sentences. Do not attempt to imitate celebrities like Salman Rushdie or V. S. Naipaul. Instead, try and follow popular and widely read authors like Khuswant Singh or James Hadley Chase.

Respect your reader and always use simple language and expression. Is there any purpose of a story in the newspaper if the reader is not able to follow what you have written? If you are not able to narrate the news in a simple and understandable language, the reader may get bored, irritated or confused. In that situation he may skip your story and read some other piece. 'Not getting read' is a great insult to a desk editor.

"English is a flexible tongue and, as headline writers and sub-editors discover, there is usually a simpler way of saying things that might at first appear and, as a rule, simplicity is the vital step on the road to clarity," suggests F. W. Hodgson, a British journalist of eminence. In journalism, an attempt to show off literary superiority and knowledge is considered disrespectful to the reader. The unknown readers might not be proficient in the language and might not be able to understand the difficult language, words and expressions being used by you. Most newspaper readers are ordinary persons having average knowledge and may not be masters of the language. They may not be as widely and highly read like you. Therefore, you should always use simple expressions that can be understood by an average reader.

Never use complicated sentences in your writing as these make even simple information difficult to understand. Simple language and expressions will ensure that the reader understands the main point or theme of the story. Acronyms and technical words should be avoided unless necessary. Jargon is only justified when it is the only right word. Trendy clichés in a news story irritate even those who do understand them.

Four—*Attract the immediate attention of the reader:* Understand that the reader does not want to spend substantial time reading your newspaper in the morning. Except retired persons, the working people can give only a short time of 20 to 30 minutes to reading the newspaper. As the pressures of life are increasing, even this time is getting shorter. Several studies have shown that the maximum time a person devotes to reading the newspaper in the morning is 15 minutes. The majority may not be spending even that much of time. Therefore, you have to get everything just right to grab the attention of the reader every morning when he is in a hurry.

The desk-editor should also be aware of the common characteristics of age, educational level, standard of living and lifestyles of the majority of the readers. The stories should be edited keeping in view the readership. The desk-editor can use flowery or rich language, if most of the readers are urban, educated and middle-class, as they can easily comprehend intricate or rich language.. Nevertheless, the general tone should be one of understandability to the reader.

Five—*Make the story communicative*: You should make the story expressive, consistent and coherent. It can be done in several ways. The most effective way is to give the main points in a summary form. These are known as bullet points and when given in an attractive way, catch the attention of the reader. An average reader scans a page and goes through the bullet points. He decides to read the whole story only when he feels that he may get useful information or the story would be interesting. If you do not care to use bullets points the reader may not care to read your story.

The desk-editor should be directed by one guiding principle: The story should be edited such, so as to make it interesting, simple and communicative. It will make the newspaper readable. It will also expand readership to those who avoid reading newspapers because they find it difficult to read and understand stories that are published.

Six—*Make the story visually attractive:* Give a good presentation to your story. The contents of a story should be presented in such a way that the story gets rooted in the psyche of the reader. The desk-editor should plan the presentation of the story in such a way so that it can attract the eye of majority of the readers. This can be achieved if the headline, text, illustrations and pictures used in the story give it a balanced shape on the page. A visually attractive story is always the first choice of every reader as it draws his attention to it. In today's competitive journalistic world, presentation is the core of the newspaper. If you make every story a visual delight, readers will like your newspaper better than others.

Seven—*Just narrate; do not try to be a preacher*: Do not preach or patronise. A newspaper does not aim to propagate an ideology, view or philosophy. Journalism is simply communicating information. A newspaper carries events of the day converted into news stories for their readers who want to know all that happened during the previous day. Therefore, you should edit the story in such a way that it does not convey the impression that you are trying to propagate some particular view. You should not pass value judgments. For example, in early January 2009, a bunch of activists under the garb of Sri Rama Sena in Karnataka, barged into a pub in Mangalore. They assaulted several young boys and girls for 'violating traditional Indian norms'. Now if this story was to be edited, the desk-editor would be required to just narrate the incident and mention the relevant details and not try to convey whether the action was right or wrong.. Some quotes of those supporting or opposing the incident can be given. But these persons must be identified. Phrases like, "These goons are not culture-bearers; they are uncivilized ruffians who have been getting a free rein under regimes ruled by the Sangh Parivar," will only go to show a personal bias. You must make sure that your story is balanced and fair. This does not mean you cannot give a view. But if you do give one viewpoint, also give adequate space to the other point of view.

Do not underestimate your reader. A newspaper reader is an intelligent person and not a dunce or simpleton. He is subscribing to your newspaper to essentially read about what happened during the past 24 hours. He does not want to listen to what is right or what is wrong. Therefore, edit the story in a balanced way and do not try to impress your opinion on the readers.

Eight—*Remain apolitical:* Newspapers are not party papers. A newspaper is subscribed and read by a large number of readers with the figure sometimes running into a few lakhs. They cannot belong to one political ideology or thinking. They have different mindsets and therefore do not want to read stories favouring any one particular political party. Therefore, the story you edit should not give a feeling that you are favouring a particular political view. Also politicians, in India particularly, are losing their credibility and respectability. Do not flatter and praise them unnecessarily. Be realistic and narrate what has happened or what they have said. Do not give more than the required space meant for them.

Nine—*Do not overwhelm the reader*: Never show off your literary superiority or richness of language to the reader. A newspaper is a matter-of-fact publication and not a literary book or treatise. If you show off your literary skills, the reader may think that you are trying to cover up the weaknesses of the story. Many times a story filed by a reporter does not carry much content. In such a situation, do not pad it by using excessive and heavy language. Cut it short and give it less space.

Make sure to simplify difficult thoughts and do not follow those desk-editors who prefer to complicate straightforward writings. Your edited story should not suffer from awful punctuation and grammatical errors. Do not let your piece become just gibberish reading.

Here is an example of the unnecessary use of complex language to overwhelm the reader:

> Hidden under layers of dust and grime at a nondescript income-tax office in Hyderabad, a can of worms in the Satyam saga is waiting to explode. A six-year-old report, buried in a labyrinth of files, maps out an intricate web of companies and *benami* bank accounts allegedly used by the disgraced Chairman of Satyam Computer, B. Ramalinga Raju and his relatives, to move money around and carry out trading in Satyam shares.

Don't try to be too clever and smart. Do not let the reader say, "God alone knows what you're saying". If you come across such a comment do not reply like many arrogant journalists do by saying, "And I doubt if he does too". You should get alarmed if you come across a comment that readers are not following you. Rather than ignoring it, you should make your stories simple and easy to understand.

Ten—*Keep on learning:* Journalism is an ever-learning profession. You come to know about new things, new people and new thinking every day. Hence, if you do not have an open mind and willingness to learn new things, your stories will lack freshness. A desk-editor should not be a highly self-satisfied person. He should not think that he is the best and most knowledgeable editor. He should be enthusiastic to learn from those who are rated high in the profession.

Desk-editors

The news desk is responsible for editing all news, articles and features that are to be published in the newspaper or the magazine. It is headed by a news editor. He is assisted by chief-sub editors, senior sub-editors and sub-editors. In many newspapers, particularly magazines, the news desk is known as copy desk. Ignoring the hierarchical order and the difference between the sub- and the copy-editor, we would use the term 'desk editor' for all those who work at the news desk.

A desk-editor is the key person in a newspaper on whose ability and efficiency the quality of the newspaper depends. The primary job of a desk-editor is to check all the written material before it goes into production. The main task is to correct errors in grammar, spelling, usage and style and also keep an eye for libel (defamatory attributions that could lead to lawsuits) and errors of facts. He may also have to rewrite the story if it is badly written or if stories from more than one source are to be merged into one. The desk-editor may also be given the additional duty to design a page. This may involve deciding which stories, pictures and graphics will be used and which of those will be featured most prominently.

The jobs that a desk-editor has to perform:

01. Check and confirm that all facts, names and places in the story are correct.
02. Check and correct all errors of grammar and spelling.
03. Edit the story in such a way that it fits into the allotted space on the page. If on the same incident, stories from more than one source are received, they have to be combined to make one composite story of the required length.
04. Attain the required balance in the story. If need be, rewrite all or part of the material to balance the different aspects of the story.
05. Check that the story, when published, would not create any legal problem. If need be it should be sent to the legal correspondent of the Bureau for opinion. If not satisfied he should bring it to the knowledge of the Editor.
06. If the material is not received online but is a written manuscript, give instructions to the key operator. Mention font size, column measure and so on so that the operator can carry them out. Mark the copy for its page, column and edition, and see that the pages of the copy are marked in correct sequence.
07. If the story is to be used for later editions, revise it in the light of latest news flow and information.
08. Provide catchy and informative captions to all pictures.
09. Give an appropriate headline to the story in the required type. It should fit in the space available.
10. Before signing off, make sure that all the above procedures have been carried out so that he can be complimented by the editor the next morning for an excellent story and not given a memo.

What is Expected From a Desk-editor?

The desk-editor is expected to perform several functions. These have been explained in detail.

Provide accuracy to the copy: It is important to make sure that the copy after editing is accurate. The desk-editor is responsible for providing an accurate copy. The reporter files a report in a great hurry and is likely to give certain facts or information incorrectly. Therefore, the desk-editor must carefully check the facts of the story and find out errors and the missing facts. The desk-editor, by nature, should be suspicious of every thing, especially the spellings of names and places. Particular care is required when dealing with well-known hyphenated names (Ban Ki-moon) or unusual spellings (Alexander Solzhenitsyn) or names like The Hague or the Philippines. Literary quotations should always be cross-checked even if sure that there is no mistake. If need be, the desk-editor should consult reference books and the clippings' file to ensure that every word is accurate. The Internet can be used for checking and cross-referencing. To check names and spellings one should go to authentic sites and not those compiled by others. If the desk-editor is not sure of certain facts or happenings, he should go back to the reporter and check with him. It is possible that he might have forgotten to include an important fact in the story. The secret of good editing is: check and check again.

The desk-editor should have an eye to detect inaccuracies. While the main thrust of a story will necessarily be taken on trust, desk-editors must check the following: names, telephone numbers, dates, registered trademarks and so on and these can be verified from printed or Internet sources or by a simple, uncontroversial telephone call. Desk-editors must have as much general knowledge and topical awareness as the reporter, and should always apply their common sense. They should, by nature, develop an attitude of questioning. Spellings should be checked too without relying too much on computer spell-checks as they only detect spelling mistakes and not the incorrect use of a word. For example, the spell-check will not indicate an error if the reporter types 'there' rather than 'their' or 'the rapists' in place of 'therapist'.

Desk-editors should approach a story from a different perspective. Reporters tend to be loyal to their sources, their interviewees and the facts of the story itself. This can mean a lack of detachment, the inclusion of too much detail and, on occasion, deliberate obscurity. Desk-editors represent the readers' interest. That means making every thing as accurate as possible. Sometimes this leads to the loss of elegance and subtlety, but that is the price that has to be paid for accuracy. Reporters and desk-editors sometimes disagree. In such a situation the matter has to be adjudicated by the Editor. Since the Editor's loyalty is also towards the readers, desk-editors generally get the Editor's support if they make the right decisions.

Ensure correct grammar and structure: Most reporters generally do not provide a good and interesting copy. They write in great hurry and so their syntax and language may not be very appropriate. They may not use the suitable and correct words. It, however, does not mean that their story is devoid of vital information and revealing facts. If the desk-editor is not sure of expressions or the language used, it must be checked with the reporter. The risk of attaching the wrong meaning should be avoided at every cost.

Wherever necessary the grammar should be simplified. If the sentence is long, it should be broken into smaller ones. When a long sentence is broken into two or more parts, the new sentence should not begin with an 'And', 'But' or 'For'. Nevertheless, the use of these conjunctions can be made for creating a desired effect. In this case, care should be taken in not using them too often. If that is not done, the desired special effect would not be created. Do not use 'dashes' in place of 'commas' thinking that they would enliven the story. 'Dashes' should be kept for genuine brackets (parentheses), and these should be few in number.

Utmost care should be used if a long sentence is broken into several sentences. A common mistake while rewriting a long sentence into small sentences is that the sequential link between the different statements gets disturbed. The corrected sentences should be read more than once and all sentences should be compared with the long sentence before deleting the old sentence. The same drill should be followed when attaching two non-sequential sentences together into one uneasy paragraph.

Always ensure that the story is correctly dated 'yesterday' or 'today' keeping in view the time the paper would appear on the street. Shortened forms such as 'can't', 'don't', 'won't', 'isn't' and 'hadn't' in an attempt to colloquialise a story should not be excessively used.

Be careful in treating a subject as singular or plural. Be consistent. Do not use 'it' and 'their' for the same thing in the same sentence.

Understand the correct usage of words. To give some examples: 'No one' and 'none' are singular. 'Different from' is correct, 'different to' is incorrect . 'Fewer than' is used and 'not less than' (of numbers) is not. 'To make a virtue of necessity' should be used and not 'make a virtue out of necessity.'

The various parts of the story must be constructed for clarity. Every thing in a story must follow logically, and there should be no internal contradictions. Having established that, the desk-editor should look at individual sentences and paragraphs to ensure that the expressions are clear. The reporter's language must be made free of padding, cliches and jargon. Every desk-editor should have a few good books on language and its usage. Some suggested books to be consulted by desk editors are: *The Oxford Dictionary for Writers & Editors* by R. M. Ritter; *Essential English for Journalists, Editors and Writers* by Harold Evans; and *Writing for Journalists* and *English for Journalists* by Wynford Hicks. Two good books that can be consulted while editing are *The King's English and Modern English Usage* and *Chambers Guide to Grammar and Usage* by George Davidson.

Avoid deviation from the house style: Every newspaper house has a style sheet. The desk-editor and, in fact, all editors should be guided by it for abbreviations and variable spellings. It will indicate whether to use 'Lt.-General' or 'Lieut-Gen'; 'Flt-Lt' or

'Flt-Lieut' and so on. It will also contain the standard short forms for states, cities, political parties and the abbreviations for trade unions and other organisations. If the date style is 19 October, dates must be written like that. Do not write October 19th. Follow the style where it spells: 'inquiry' not 'enquiry', 'dispatch' not 'despatch', 'organise' not 'organize'. If the British English spellings are to be followed, never use the American spellings. Never use mixed spellings—English at one place and American at another. A careful desk-editor will soon find that he knows exactly what the style is without referring to the style sheet and the consistency will be achieved.

Edit the story to fit in the allotted place: Every reporter wants to give the maximum information and facts that he has collected, which makes them write long stories. The desk-editor has to edit every report that is filed, with a judicious mind and a professional attitude. His main job is to edit the story and remove the flab so that it fits exactly in the allotted space. This process is known as 'casting off'. It comes from a printing term meaning, to cast a line of metal type to an exact fit.

Desk-editors will often make substantial cuts in submitted stories or carry out major rewrites. If the changes are extensive, the reporter should be informed. Shortening a story or article by deleting words can lead to changing the whole theme, episode or characters rather than mere tinkering. You should get in touch with the reporter to know which parts he would like to come through the process. The standard practice should be to work on computer copies rather than on the originals, as the option of returning to the original form of words must always be available.

A good desk-editor will ensure that the story begins in an interesting way. As a matter of habit, it must be ensured that the central point of the story, known as 'news peg' appears in the introductory paragraph. In the journalistic parlance it is known as 'intro'. When the desk-editor is satisfied that the intro is interesting, he can cast off the story by following two methods: pruning words and pruning facts.

Word pruning requires that all superfluous words and phrases be removed from the story in such a way that every remaining word is meaningful. This can be done by removing unnecessary adjectives. The quotes can be shortened to the minimum length. However, it has to be ensured that what the person wants to convey is not mutilated.

Fact pruning is to delete those facts that are not very relevant to the story. First the least important facts should be taken out. Work back and keep on eliminating till you have the length that can fit into the allotted space. A good newspaper should train its reporters and correspondents to write every story in such a way that the last few paragraphs can be knocked down without damaging the story. If that can be done, the work of the desk editor will be easier. Since not many stories are written that way, do not prune the story blindly. If the reporter has narrated the main story in the last few paragraphs, your doing so will destroy the entire story. So the desk editor should first read the whole story and then rearrange it after removing those parts that can be easily deleted.

An efficient desk-editor, before beginning to edit the story, would first find out the exact space allotted to the story. He would then find out the number of words required. An imaginative desk-editor would keep some specimen column inches from the newspaper in various fonts in use. He can easily find out the number of words once he comes to know the space allotted to the story. Thus, if one column length in 8pt Times Roman takes 40 words to the column-inch, the sub would know that a 5-inch story for page 5 would require 200 words.

The technique is the same if the material is from several sources, i.e. may be from two reporters, a news agency and a few stringers in different cities. The story still has to be cast off to fit in the space; though in the case of some running stories—stories that last over a period—it might be worth asking for more space if the desk-editor thinks that the material is better than was expected.

Rewrite the story if required: The desk-editor may have to rewrite the whole story if it is poorly written; though, this should be avoided as far as possible. But it may be necessary for coherence where a story is written in bad language with no syntax, with the facts in wrong sequence or where a story is collated from several sources. In many cases rewriting is required for certain portions of the story, usually the intro and first part. However, the desk editor has to take an on-the-spot decision whether a complete re-write is required. A lot of experience and expertise is required in rewriting a story. Some desk-editors possess special rewriting skills.

Rewriting should only take place when it is a must. A commissioned article should be published as the author wrote it. If some changes are essential, the author may be requested to include them in his piece. But once the author has provided a second draft, it should not be changed. Features that are written specially for the newspaper are prized for their style, which may be more courageous than would be acceptable on a news page. Desk-editors should not change the language or the order.

Legal check: Apart from accuracy and grammar, the desk-editor must ensure that the story when published will not cause any legal complications, ending in lengthy and expensive litigation. A reporter is enthusiastic to give revealing facts and information and in that excitement forgets about the legal complication it might create. Skill and concentration is an essential quality in a desk-editor to watch for such traps in a story that may basically seem simple and well written. The desk-editor should never relax his vigilance while signing off a story.

The desk-editors should also spot defamatory and potentially actionable statements. Libel cases often come about due to an accident. Any critical statement about any living person, company, product or organisation can be potentially troublesome. Desk editors should get into the habit of asking, "Would I like this written about me?" If not, then there is likely to be a problem.

Every desk-editor should have an elementary knowledge of libel, contempt of court, privileges, and the effects of the

Official Secrets Act. If any aspect of the story requires extra legal expertise, it should be sent to the legal correspondent or the legal consultant of the newspaper. If the story is not legally safe, the legal correspondent or the consultant will advise that the story should not be carried. It then, should be refereed to the Editor for his final decision. If only part of it is legally unsafe, the desk-editor, under legal advice should edit the story in such a way that it becomes legally safe. It can also be sent to the reporter for further checks and information so that the story does not lose its punch.

Instructions: If the desk-editor is not editing the copy online, the manuscript should be marked indicating the required font, its size and column size. He should also mark the page, column and edition for which it is intended. The pages of the copy should be marked in correct identifiable sequence so that the story can be collated either in the composing room or on the computer. This is also required when the copy is to be keyed in by the data key operator.

Thus the desk-editor might mark a single column top at the head of the first page, in the space left, 'Page 7. Col. 6, 2nd edn.' Under this mark and at the head of each successive folio will be marked the body type and width. Perhaps the first paragraph will be marked '10pt x double column'; the second paragraph '8pt x single column' and each successive folio '7pt x single column'.

Each page must have a clear catch line, i.e. the first page, for instance, might read '# 1,' the second folio '# 2' and so on until the last page which should be marked 'end' at the bottom or just a # sign. Any change of setting during a story, i.e. from a double column intro to single column body, must be clearly marked on the copy.

In choosing a catch line a commonplace one like 'rob' for a robbery story should be avoided since there could be another robbery story. If the second story too has the same catch line, there would be confusion. The catch line should, however, be a syllable of a word relating to the story.

Revision: The story should be revised after editing is completed. The desk-editor may have to check if some more facts have arrived that may alter or improve the story for a later edition, or because the position of the story on a page has been changed for a later edition and it has to be shortened or lengthened. After modification a new catch line should be given.

Giving a caption: Every picture which is used along with a story should be given a caption. Even when a picture is used independently, a caption is a must. The caption should explain the subject of the picture. From the caption point of view, stories can be of two types: self-contained stories that are developed around the subject of the picture; and, stories where pictures are used only to illustrate the story.

Writing a caption to a picture for a *self-contained story* is not a simple job. It requires great skill, specialisation and experience. It gives scope for whimsy and imagination since it often has to establish a justification for using a picture that may be decorative or visually attractive rather than newsworthy.

A *line-caption* is simply for identification when picture is used only to illustrate the story; although, a quotation or a news point can be used where possible. For example, there is a picture of a road accident. The accident was between a stationary truck and a motor cycle. The person on the motor cycle, Rohit did not see the truck and hit it. He fell down and the motor cycle was badly damaged. Fortunately Rohit got only a few bruises. He is shown standing shocked along with the damaged motor cycle. The desk-editor suggested the following two captions, both of which were considered good. The second caption was approved for use.

AFTER the accident: Rohit
Or
ROHIT: "I am lucky to be alive".

Newspapers follow a general rule universally that no picture, even if it is closely identified with a story, is to be used without a caption. A reader is almost certain to see the picture first and should know who or what it is about.

Captions are there to label the elements in a picture, but not to describe them. Those who write captions should ensure that they know exactly what the picture shows and be careful not to state the obvious. The caption should, whenever possible, add something to the picture that the visual cannot convey. There is no need to say 'This picture shows...' You can safely omit the obvious. Readers do expect to know the identities of the people in a picture. If you don't have their names or you do not think they are relevant, you need to find a way to explain them. Desk-editors must also check that the correct photographs are being used. Confusing two people with similar names can be a costly error if one is a known criminal and the other is a blameless professor.

> **Sub-editing**
>
> Sub-editing involves three tasks:
>
> **Quality control:** To make sure that everything that goes in the story is accurate, well written and legally safe.
>
> **Production:** To make sure that everything fits into the allotted space and that deadlines are met.
>
> **Presentation:** To present the whole story to create maximum effect, through headlines, introduction and captions.

Desk-editor and Production

A newspaper's schedule allocates time for all the editorial tasks, from initial commissioning, to research, desk editing and layout. The desk-editors have to enforce the schedule from the very beginning. They have to ensure that the copy arrives on time and pages leave on dot. Delay costs money. The desk-editors would always receive an Editor's support in their struggle to enforce deadlines. They are also responsible for keeping control of copy-flow, ensuring that the correct files come in and go out. A logical structure of file names is important here, as is a system to log traffic between the editorial office and the outside facilities. Desk-editors must understand the editorial computer programs and system inside out.

Along with sending material online, desk-editors should also read the hard copy, as far as possible. The reason is that many errors can be detected on paper than on the screen. In addition to checking for typographical errors and missing lines and words, desk editors must watch out for wrong fonts, use of upper and lower cases, and font sizes, all of which are easy to do but hard to spot, in layout programmes.

It is usual for desk-editors to handle copy editing as well as page layout in those professional magazines that use newspaper-style layout. They have a key role in the projection of editorial material. It really helps them if they receive proper training to do this job. It is better if even those desk-editors who are not involved in the visual aspect of the magazine also have some responsibility for writing words that project the editorial matter. They have to persuade people to read. That means writing strong cover-lines, headlines, introductions and captions. The Editor should keep an eye on quality and should set the pattern. This, however, does not mean stamping out individual motivation.

All of this will probably be done at a computer screen using panoply of software packages, each of which the subeditor must be able to use, although wise subs will still leave some room on their desks for paper.

In the end, it can definitely be said that desk-editors are an integral part of a newspaper organisation. They have to check the correspondent's copy for grammatical and factual mistakes and reduce or expand the copy to the required size, write headlines and give captions to pictures. Desk-editors not only correct spelling and grammar, they also check factual accuracy, rewrite copy to make it better or to fit in with the house style, seek out potential libels and remove them, fit copy into a layout, and devise headlines, introductions and captions. All of this is done at a computer screen using various software packages, though intelligent desk-editors still depend on hard copies.

They are the ones who make the page look good, to convey the weight and sense of its contents clearly and to provide a text free from linguistic impediments. They are the invisible figures behind the success or failure of a newspaper. Therefore desk-editors have to be a product of solid skills, high level of education and awareness, and sharp verbal intelligence. These skills can be acquired through proper training and experience. These are the two that distinguish a good desk-editor from a bad one.

References:

Many Voice, One World, Report by the International Commission for the Study of Communication Problems, (UNESCO, Kogan Page, London/ Unipub, New York/Unesco, Paris).

Five Hundred Years of Printing, S. H. Steinberg, (British Library).

Journalism in India, Rangaswami Parthasarathy (Sterling Publishers Private Limited, New Delhi)

The New University One-volume Encyclopedia, Editor-in-Chief, Franklin Dunham (J.J. Little & Ives Co. Inc., New York)

Modern Newspaper Practice, F. W. Hodgson (Heinemann: London)

Subediting for Journalists, Wynford Hicks and Tim Holmes (Routledge).

3

Editing Prerequisites

Editing is a great job. It is a challenging task. You work every day, round the year, to make news stories, articles and features interesting and newsworthy for your readers. What you receive is mainly raw material. Much of it may be unreadable, verbose, lengthy and difficult to understand. You have to cut and rewrite every piece so that the complex information is provided in a clear and concise manner to the readers and in a language that is simple enough for most of them to understand. You have to fit every piece in the allotted space so that the whole page looks attractive. Your job can be compared to that of an accomplished costume designer, who has to cut and fit the dress on a body so that it looks attractive. A desk-editor, similarly, attempts to fit every story on the body of every page so that the whole newspaper looks well proportioned and attractive.

Points to Remember

Your Objective:
every reader should be
able to read and understand
what the story conveys.

Fundamental Rules a Desk-editor Needs to Follow

IDENTIFY THE NEWS PEG

The first fundamental rule of editing is to read the whole story quickly and find out what is the most important piece of news in it. 'The most important part in the story' is known as the news peg or the central point. The news peg is defined in terms of:
1. Breadth and depth of impact.
2. What is the most current?
3. What is the most interesting?

In brief, you have to find out what makes the story newsworthy. Your first action should be to read the whole piece and identify the main focus of the story. It should be unique as several stories may be discussing the same topic.

Let us take an example. Suppose there is a plane crash on the runway at the Delhi airport. Several stories may be given for editing regarding the accident. Your correspondents may file some and some others may be from different news agencies. Each of the stories will have a different news peg. One story may describe that how during a short period of 30 minutes the weather conditions changed so drastically that while other airplanes landed safely only this one crashed. The central point of this story may be, *'rain played havoc with flight conditions.'*
The second story may describe what happened in the passenger cabin and how passengers faced the situation and how those who survived helped others and made to safety. Its focus may be, *'the courage shown by passengers and the flight crew.'* The third story may describe the reaction of the airport authorities in fighting the accident at the airport. It may describe how soon the fire brigade reached, how the fire fighting team tackled the accident, and how speedily the medical facilities were provided to the passengers. Its news peg can be *'Airport Authority's reaction to the crash.'*

Here all stories are about the plane crash on the runway but each one has a distinct central point or focus and provides information relevant to exactly that.

Editing Prerequisites

Sometimes the story may have more than one central point. In such a situation the editor has to depend on his news judgment skills. The selection of the central point may also depend on what would be of maximum interest to the readers of the newspaper.

> Identifying the news peg in the beginning is of utmost importance. If that is not done the story may become incoherent.

The central point should be communicated in the first paragraph of the story. The purpose of doing this is to tell the reader how important the story is. Also, what they would know after reading the whole piece.

An example of a story without focus:

A question mark hangs over the fate of National Commission for Women (NCW) member Nirmala Venkatesh after the Commission rejected her report on the Mangalore pub attack. Venkatesh is a former member of the Karnataka Legislative Council. She said, when contacted, that she stood by her report. She also refused to resign from her position. Venkatesh was issued a show cause notice by the Ministry Women and Child Development (WCD) on Thursday for dereliction of duty and acting against public interest. She is expected to reply to the notice by Monday. It is being said that WCD minister Renuka Choudhary will consider various options, including dismissing Venkatesh. According to the NCW Act, a member can only be removed if she has acted against public interest. In such a case, acting on the WCD minister's recommendation, the PM can ask for the member's resignation.

It is being surmised that, the ministry gave a notice to Venkatesh after NCW chairperson Girija Vyas had submitted a report on its member to the WCD ministry. Vyas, in her letter, has reportedly expressed dissatisfaction over Venkatesh's conduct in Mangalore and her general conduct with the staff. Vyas on Friday clarified that since the report was found "inadequate" on certain parameters, it would not be accepted by the Commission and will instead be considered as an individual's opinion. She said Venkatesh had not spoken to the victims and had involved herself in the pub's licensing issues, a matter that was not part of the terms of reference of the inquiry. Vyas said, "The Commission has always fought for women's rights. We have found the member's report lacking in certain aspects and so we have not accepted it."

Venkatesh had led a two-member team to inquire into the January 24 attack on girls and boys at a pub in Mangalore by a self-styled moral brigade of Hindu outfit Sri Ram Sene. In her report she blamed the pub owners for the incident saying they had not provided enough security. Apparently unhappy with Venkatesh's comments, the WCD minister had dispatched another enquiry team. She also issued a show cause notice to the NCW member for not submitting her report on time. A defiant Venkatesh stuck to her guns. When asked if she would resign after the adverse remarks from the NCW chairperson and WCD ministry, Venkatesh said, "Why should I resign? If there is a notice, I will explain my stand."

Meanwhile, All India Democratic Women's Association (AIDWA) has condemned Sri Ram Sene chief Pramod Muthalik's threats against couples celebrating Valentine's Day. "The fascist threats that are being issued (couples found going out together would be forced to tie the *mangalsutra*, women wearing particular type of clothes would be assaulted, and so on), are a gross violation of fundamental rights, and pose a grave threat to our democratic polity. The Karnataka state government must act immediately and make sure that the lives and rights of the citizens of our country are safeguarded," Suhasini Ali, AIDWA President, said in a statement.

Editing Prerequisites 35

Choudhary's remarks on organising a "pub bharo" andolan to defy the moral brigade have come under fire from NGOs. Rishikant from Shakti Vahini said, "As a man working for women's rights, I am deeply offended by the Union Minister's attempt to trivialise a serious issue. The solution for women being beaten up in full public gaze is not to rush to pubs. This will turn more men against the women's cause."

Now the same story with focus:

The National Commission for Women (NCW) has rejected the report submitted by its probe team member Nirmala Venkatesh on the Mangalore pub attack. NCW Chairperson Girija Vyas found the report faulty on several counts. The most important was that it failed to denounce the attack on college girls. Instead it focused on pub security and its licences. The probe team also 'lacked' a vital member—a social activist—as part of the inquiry team and failed to interact with any of the victims. She also found the language of the report submitted by Venkatesh, who is herself from Karnataka, bizarre.

Venkatesh was asked to investigate the actions of the self-styled pro-Hindu moral brigade called Sri Rama Sena that had barged into a pub in Mangalore on January 24. The girls in the pub were molested for "violating traditional Indian norms."

The report observed, "The incident occurred while stopping the semi-nude dancing under the influence of alcohol and drugs it was told." It further stated that the probe team made all efforts to trace the victims but it was not possible "since all the girls ran away from Mangalore." In her recommendations, instead of suggesting stringent action against the Sri Rama Sena, Venkatesh observed that, "All citizens have the right to form associations and unions." She also said that it is the job of the government to decide which body to ban. She blamed the pub for the incident for not providing adequate security to girls. She suggested strict vigilance on pubs and hotels.

"The committee did not meet any of the victims and merely said they could not be contacted," said Vyas. Also, it reportedly raided Hotel Siddhartha, the reasons for which are not clear. The Ministry of Women and Child Development (WCD), while issuing a show cause notice to Venkatesh on Thursday, had cited "delay in submission of the report" as a major reason. Vyas herself had complained to the Ministry about Venkatesh's delay on the report.

It was commonly known that the report would not be accepted because Vyas had distanced herself from it on February 2, when it was submitted to MCW. Earlier to that, Venkatesh publicly made her views known against the pub owners, which had embarrassed the commission and hardened the case against her. The final blow was Venkatesh's outburst against WCD minister Renuka Chowdhury before the media, when she questioned, "Who is Renuka Chowdhury?"

Venkatesh, however, remained adamant and refused to apologise. "I will not apologise for a wrong I have not done," she said on Friday. Vyas was silent on the show cause notice being served to Venkatesh and says it is the WCD ministry's affairs. Meanwhile, a two-member team of the WCD ministry, probing the attack, submitted its report to Chowdhury on Friday. The report said the girls were "indeed molested without provocation" and blamed the administration.

Simplify the Language

The second essential of news editing is to keep the language simple, always. Fancy, hyperbolic and un-understandable words should not be used in a news story. Always prefer one- or two- syllable words as these are shorter and simpler. The word 'use' should be preferred instead of 'utilise', 'built' rather than 'construct', 'spit' instead of 'expectorate', 'rather' instead of 'approximately', 'home' and not 'residence' 'call' rather than 'summon'.

Some expressions that a good desk-editor should prefer:

Use	*Avoid*
About	Around
Aeroplane	Aircraft or airplane
Among	Amongst
And so on	Etc.
Begin	Commence
Burnt	Burned
Commoner	Hoi polloi
Continuous	Continual
Deny	Rebut
Emigrant	Expatriate
Enough	Sufficient
Group	Cohort
Horrible	Grisly
Inchoate	Indistinct
Kill	Decimate
Means	Entail
Now	Currently
Often	Regularly
People	Folks
Sacred	Holy
Spoken	Verbal

The reasons for maintaining simplicity in the language are many. Simple language is used because it is closer to everyday speech than academic or business writing. It also improves the clarity of the story to the reader. If you do not have clarity you lose your readers as they are unable to understand your complex and difficult language. Roy Peter Clark of the Poynter Institute for Media Studies believes, "The most valued quality of the language of journalism is clarity, and its most desired effect is to be understood." Clarity can be achieved by using a simple language and writing understandable paragraphs. Remember what Winston Churchill used to say: "Knowledge isn't worth much if we can't convey it to others."

The sentences and paragraphs need to be kept short. The reason is that short sentences are easy to read and comprehension is quick. Short sentences are also more lucid and effective and do not distract the reader; facts too can be emphasised clearly and forcefully with short sentences. Reporters are usually in the habit of writing long and uncoordinated sentences. The desk-editors should rewrite long and awkward sentences into short and understandable ones. It has been found that majority of the newspaper readers can easily understand a sentence having an average of 20 words. As the sentence becomes longer, the possibility of its understandability declines fast.

This, however, does not mean that sentences should always be short. It all depends on the subject and the context. Sometimes a long sentence is required to break the monotony of reading. Too many short sentences in a row will make the story shabby. A good desk-editor will know when the story is becoming jerky due to the short sentences and will add one long sentence. Carefully constructed long sentences will make the story extremely effective. However, care has to be taken that the sentences do not become too long and complex. But too many long sentences will make the reading quite awkward. It would also be difficult to understand and comprehend the story.

There is a reason for sentences and paragraphs to be short in the newspaper. Newspapers are printed in small types, narrow columns and on newsprint. Also readers are in a hurry to read the news. They want to scan the paper and get the most of the news in the minimum possible time. If the paragraphs are long and the sentences complex, readers may be discouraged to go through the stories. From the design point of view also short paragraphs give a better look. Spaces left at the ends of paragraphs provide breathing space and also brighten each page.

Ideally, if time permits, a story should be tested for lucidity and comfortable reading. It helps to consult your senior editors for understanding and rewriting of complicated and long sentences. Reading the story 'aloud' to yourself can do this. Listen with closed eyes the natural rhythm or flow of words and sentences. If you find a sentence sounding awkward or inappropriate rewrite it using simple words and phrases.

Here are two examples of how to shorten sentences:

Earlier: Both faculty and students undertook planning for a new class schedule.

Revised: Faculty and students planned a new class schedule.

Earlier: Left paralysed on the left side of his body after brain surgery last summer, the 22-year old boy is suing his doctor for two crore rupees compensation.

Revised: The 22-year old boy is suing his doctor for two crore rupees.

He has been paralysed on his left side since brain surgery last summer.

How to Achieve Simplicity?

01. Always try to use subject-verb-object.

    Your sentence should have a subject
    (the person or the thing in action), a verb (the action) and
    a direct object (the person or thing acted upon).

Examples:

The robber knew his address.
The boy has lost his way.
The rich should help the poor.

02. Use active verbs.

    The verb (action) should be attributed directly to the person.

Examples:

The lady slapped the traffic cop;
not
The traffic cop was slapped by the lady.

The pickpocket stabbed the victim.
not
The victim was stabbed by the pickpocket.

03. Do not use complicated words. Reduce them to as little as possible and change them into single or simple words.

Examples:

To call it quits	to quit
Painted a rosy picture	praised
Geared towards	designed for

04. Be specific and not theoretical.

    Do not use general terms. Be specific.

    Keep your sentences short.

    But the length of different sentences should be different and not same.

05. Do not use too much data because not many are able to follow it.

    Too much data may confuse the reader.

06. Avoid too many prepositions.

Understand the Story

First try to understand the story thoroughly. If you yourself do not understand the piece that you are editing, your readers will also not be able to comprehend the story. Also, if you cannot assimilate the story, the whole exercise of editing would be irrelevant and superfluous. It would merely involve adding or dropping a few words here and there and giving to your readers something that may not look like a story. Whereas, if you yourself fully understand the story, then you would also be able to make it comprehendible for your readers.

If you want the readers to understand the story, avoid using technical words and jargon. As they do not have mastery over the subject they can never understand such words. All technical words and jargon should be written in simple language which is used in every day life.

Secondly, quotations should be made understandable. Most of the quotations given to reporters are not properly worded and therefore fail to make sense. They should be edited and made comprehendible. If need be the quotations may be shortened and fitted into the text. If that is not possible the quotation marks can be deleted.

Thirdly, abbreviations and acronyms should not be used without expanding them in the beginning where they occur for the first time. Many readers may not be familiar with these usages and may wonder what they stand for. It need not be expanded if the acronym is widely used, for example Noida which is extensively used than its full form (New Okhla Industrial Development Authority) which is not known to the people and is rarely used. But every abbreviation should be expanded when it is used for the first time in the text and should be given in brackets. After that it should be used as a word. Whether it should be used as all-caps or upper-lower or all-lower depends on the style that the newspaper has decided to follow. For example: United Nations Educational, Scientific and Cultural Organisation can be written as UNESCO or Unesco or unesco, as per the style followed by the newspaper.

A good desk-editor is also a good storyteller. For that you should make the story understandable even to an amateur. Remove every word or expression that is irrelevant or is difficult to understand.

Remove Unnecessary Words

Desk-editors are wordsmiths. They cut off words like the best hedge cutter. They do not waste the time of the reader nor the space in the newspaper by using two or three words, when only one is needed. They know the appropriate word for the expression and use it. The reporter may not do that for the simple reason that he writes the story in a great hurry. Most of the reporters more often than not do that because they file stories in haste. They, therefore, do not want to waste time on using the language correctly. You must learn that art and should not use words that are not needed. The story should be so edited that it becomes precise and explicit. However, it should be detailed enough to be informative.

Editing to make the story short and concise is necessary for the simple reason that every newspaper is short of space. Each day the newspaper receives ten to twenty times more material than it can publish. It can use only a fraction of information received. By making stories concise, editors can enable the newspaper to carry more information. It would give the reader the satisfaction of being better informed than others are.

Achieve Accuracy

Accuracy should be an editor's first objective. If accuracy is lacking, the readers will lose faith in the newspaper. Even a small error weakens the readers' confidence. If factual errors are committed or important information is missed, the newspaper loses its credibility.

Accuracy means many things. Meticulous efforts have to be made in mentioning facts, data and figures. The information should be correct and facts should not conflict. The names of the people, places and countries should be spelled out correctly.

Editing Prerequisites

Tips to Learn Concise Writing

01. Some words become obsolete with the passage of time. These do not remain in common use and convey nothing much and are unnecessary additions to a sentence. Some of these words are 'that', 'then', 'currently', 'now', and 'presently'.

02. It is not necessary to add a second word to reiterate the time when the verb tense and the noun indicate when the action happened.

Some examples are:
'*Past* history',   '*is* now'   '*future* plans'.

03. Redundant words, that merely repeat the same idea, should be avoided. In the following phrases the word/words in italics is/are not required as the remaining word fully conveys the idea.

The *only* gunman   *physical* injury   fallen *down*
New innovation   *at this time* provides   *past* happenings
Assisted *onward*   *end* result   *bodily* pain

04. Superfluous words should be removed without changing the meaning:

Earlier: He was able to drive his mother to the mall.

Revised: He drove his mother to the mall.

Earlier: This is not the first time she has been attacked. She has been attacked three times in the past six months.

Revised: She has been attacked three times in the past six months.

Misspelling the name of a person, more so if he is well known is not only flawed but is discourteous. It is offensive and insulting to the person. Using wrong spellings not only shows neglect and misdemeanor but the news story also becomes clumsy.

If the story carries addresses, they must be double-checked and verified from different sources. Special care must be taken when telephone numbers are given. Any mistake can be damaging. The number given will get incessant calls and the person would be unnecessarily disturbed and harassed. Readers will be greatly inconvenienced and will hold the newspaper responsible if the place and time of an event, say a play, is wrongly mentioned.

Desk-editors have to make their system and develop their own sources for achieving accuracy. They should not depend on anyone else for getting the right information and cross-checking facts, figures and information. A desk-editor therefore has to develop the habit of becoming a doubter of his own work. You have to become your own critic. Double-checking should become your second habit.

Accuracy also means that there should not be a contradiction in the story. There should not be two facts or information opposing each other. For example when you mention 10 billion in the opening paragraph and after a few paragraphs repeat it as 10 million you are contradicting yourself in the story you edited. Such mistakes are very common and can be taken care of if the desk-editors cross-check the repeated figures or names after they finish editing their piece. Here is an example of contradiction and careless editing in a story published in a widely circulated newspaper that came out one Saturday morning:

> New Delhi: Seeking a rollback of all reservations based on caste by the government, members of Youth for Equality will march from Maulana Azad Medical College on Bahadur Shah Zafar Marg to Jantar Mantar on Wednesday. The protest march is expected to cause disruption of traffic in central Delhi and motorists are advised to avoid it.

The rally is scheduled to start at 9 a.m. from MAMC. Protesting medial students will march via Jawaharlal Nehru Marg, Ranji flyover, Barakhamba Road, Tolstoy Marg, Sansad Marg to reach Jantar Mantar.

The march is expected to slow down movement of traffic at ITO, Delhi Gate, Tilak Marg, Sikandra Road, Vikas Marg, Subhash Marg, and Asaf Ali Marg. "Though it is being organised on a Saturday afternoon, it might lead to some congestion in the area," said a senior traffic police official.

(Saturday afternoon and 9 a.m. is a contradiction. Probably it was morning and because of a subbing error it became afternoon.)

You can be a good desk-editor if you always keep in mind four tips. *One*, always check numbers; if there is any suspicion consult the original source. *Two*, ensure that every name is spelled correctly. Do not treat the names of persons being mentioned in the story lightly. Treat every name with respect and consider it sacred. *Three*, if you have any doubt about any fact, figure, or information, do not use it. It is better to drop it rather than face trouble later. *Four*, do not depend on anyone else to carry out your checking for you. It is your responsibility and only you should see that the accuracy is maintained. If you fail, you are responsible for it and not anyone else.

Journalists with a long experience in the profession advise that all spellings, figures and other statements must be checked against reliable printed sources. Over time you should develop a small reference library that should be kept up to date. The Internet should be frequently, but carefully, used. But you should double check from other sources of reference. Quotes must always be exact. This is more important in a newspaper. A much higher level of accuracy is required when things appear in print than is normal in day-to-day gossip and chit-chat, where it is quite acceptable to say things that are not true or exact.

Remain Objective

News stories should be impartial and objective. Since every reporter has his own leanings, the natural tendency is to interpret news and give his own perception. Such correspondents just do not report what happened at the scene of occurrence. They interpret the news and provide their own viewpoint on it. But this is not real or legitimate news reporting. In fact, views and interpretations should be confined to the editorials, news analyses, commentaries and articles. A news report should be free from opinions and should be as dispassionate and objective as possible. If the reporter has not done this job, the desk editor has to do it to be fair to the readers. He should edit the story in a manner that facts are presented fairly and all sides are written in a balanced way. Every story should be made free of opinion and it should not be an advocate of one view. It should be so edited that it becomes neutral. Objectivity is one of the cardinal principles of journalism. "I had to report the happenings as they unfolded, good or bad, without letting my feelings cloud my judgment", wrote eminent Indian journalist, Kuldeep Nayar in his book *Scoop*.

A desk-editor must understand that news writing is different from academic or political writing. A reporter draws on the public. He talks to various people, interest groups and political leaders. All this investigation provides him with the ideas and information. He filters those ideas and information and then writes a news story. It is edited, published and read by the very people who gave the information. The views expressed by various persons should be attributed to them. Attributions give credibility to the story as readers get to know about the source of information. Also it makes the person who gave the information responsible for it and not the newspaper or the reporter. However, there is no scope for personal opinion. If at all it is to be used, it should be used very judiciously.

While attributing information, the name and position of the person should be given. The relationship between the name and position should not be assumed as understood, even of important persons. The newspaper is accepted as the primary source for research. Therefore, a researcher might be using this information after 50 years and the person may not be known at that time.

The desk-editor can adopt several techniques to make a story neutral and free from biases. First, slanted word like 'demagogue', 'radical', 'unsophisticated', 'fanatic', 'crank person', 'barbarous' should be avoided. Words like these are unnecessary cliché. They usually convey committed meaning that is not very positive. Besides being adage, such words may not be liked by those who hold opposite views. Secondly, avoid using expressions that may look like opinions; for example 'the discussion was *heated*', 'the death was *unfortunate*', 'he murdered the person *violently*, 'he was an *alert* witness,' 'it was a *gala* reception.' The italicised words indicate opinion and should be avoided.

However, the story can tell readers what to think about—what is important. They need information to take decisions on matters that affect their lives. Also opinions expressed by others can be quoted. But these must be attributed to those who expressed that opinion. If that is not done the readers may think that it is the opinion of the newspaper.

An example of a not-so-well-edited story

Given here are two stories on the same news peg. The first one is poorly edited, as it does not clearly state the news peg. It is a story on Sanjay Chandvani, Chairman of Chandvani Industries Limited, objecting to a certain deal by his brother, Vijay Chandvani with Malaysia-based telecom giant to sell shares of CCOM. One is not clear what the main point of dispute is. It only gives an indication that it is the clause of first-purchase. But what is that clause remains unclear. Though it can be understood by most readers, a well-edited story should be very clear and specific about the main cause of contention. The edited story goes like this:

> There are early signs of gruesome renewal of war between the Chandvani brothers. This time the cause may be Vijay Chandvani's Chandvani Communications' merger talks with Malaysia based telecom giant KLCC.

[This is a long and confusing sentence and there should not be two apostrophes so close by.]

News leaked out Friday evening, that Sanjay Chandvani-led Chandvani Industries Limited (CIL), which had reluctantly parted with its telecom business when the brothers split, had written to the KLCC board informing them about a clause in the family settlement which reserves first right for refusal for Sanjay Chandvani or his companies. [Again a long sentence has been written that is complicated and does not clarify what the writer wants to convey.]

CCOM immediately hit back with a mocking statement, saying, "Last night, in a mala fide effort to disrupt talks, CIL, part of the Sanjay Chandvani Group, has sent a communication to KLCC Group, making a false claim of an alleged right of first refusal to buy controlling stake in CCOM. Not surprisingly, CIL has sent the letter to CCOM only today that is after a gap of 24 hours."

CCOM continued to state, "CIL's claim is not tenable legally and factually. It is baseless and misconceived and is born out of mounting despair and frustration at CCOM Group's continuing successes. CIL is seeking to destroy the possibility of the creation of one of the world's most valuable telecom combinations, which will make over a billion Indians proud of our generation."

"CIL's actions are clearly anti-consumer, anti-investor and anti-globalization and against the vision of our father. CCOM dismisses CIL's claims with the disdain it is worthy of."

The story has not been skillfully edited. It caries too many quotes from the press release of the company. Apart from being complex, the extensive use of quotes indicates the possibility of the story being a plant. The story is complex because of long sentences and the usage of too many apostrophes. If the long sentences are divided into small sentences, comprehension will become easy and smooth.

An example of a well-edited story

The same morning another popular national broadsheet carried the story that was better edited. The story goes like this:

The Vijay Chandvani Group (VCG) on Friday alleged that Sanjay Chandvani's, Chandvani Industries Ltd. (CIL) was trying to "disrupt" the ongoing merger talks between Chandvani Communications Ltd. (RCOM) and Malasia's telecom major KLCC.

The charge signalled a fresh spat between the Chandvani brothers who split the family business between themselves in 2005. CCOM, founded and nurtured by Sanjay, went to Vijay as a part of the settlement.

Sources said, CIL company secretary S. Ramachandra wrote to KLCC on June 12, saying CIL had a "first right to refusal" on the shares of CCOM. The deal structure planned between KLCC and CCOM suggests that while the promoter's holding in CCOM' will be transferred to KLCC, the promoters of KLCC will transfer their holding to Vijay Chandvani.

CIL's spokesman said: "CIL has in good faith notified both Vijay Chandvani Group and KLCC Group of stipulations contained in an agreement, the validity for which has never been questioned so far by VCG."

A release from VCG late on Friday said, CIL had claimed the right to buy the shares of CCOM promoters in case they wanted to sell. CIL was making this claim on the basis of an agreement between Chandvani Communication Ventures Ltd. and CIL, signed on February 08, 2006," it added.

Chandvani Communication Ventures was one of the vehicles

used to demerge the shareholding in telecom business of CIL.

This story is well edited. It is focused and explains all the aspects of the dispute clearly. It does not use too many quotes from the press release and the sentences used are short and clear.

> **Points to Remember**
>
> Ensure there is focus in the story.
> Use short words that readers can easily understand.
> Use simple sentences that follow normal word order:
> subject-verb-direct-object.
> Keep paragraphs short.
> > Delete words that are not needed.
> > Do not use expressions that are opinions of reporters.
> > Do not overload sentences with unrelated words.
> > Accuracy should be your first goal.
> > Anything that should be checked must be checked.

Exercise

The city reporter filed a story. The Editor wants to use it. Read it carefully and answer the following questions:

1. Your editor finds it a good human-interest story and decides to use it. He sends it to you for editing. Edit the story in 200 words.
2. Give a proper headline to the story.
3. Write a lead to the story.

The story

> A child's corpse went missing from his grave hours after his burial on Tuesday, fuelling rumours of *a tantrik's* involvement.
>
> Three-month-old Kaku, son of Madhavpuram resident Rahul Sharma, died on Tuesday. The body was buried in the Surajkund Children grave yard around 11 a.m. When family members went to the grave at night to perform some rituals, they were shocked to find the grave dug up and the body missing. Distraught family members informed the police. Most people living near the burial ground blamed stray dogs and pigs.

But a report in an evening newspaper, hinting at the involvement of a *tantrik* claimed that bodies of at least 20 children were missing from their graves under suspicious circumstances. The police has denied the report but said they were investigating the charge. "So far we have not found any evidence of *tantrik* being behind the incident,' a police officer said.

Local residents blame the authorities for allowing the graveyard to turn into a haunt for animals. "Dogs and pigs often dig out corpses from the graves," said Naresh. He said he had often had to scare away animals feeding on corpses. The Municipal Corporation is looking after the burial ground.

Mayor has assured the people that the graveyard would be given a facelift. Expressing grief over the incident he held the district administration equally responsible for the condition of the graveyard. He said officials have been ordered to raise the boundary wall to stop the entry of dogs and pigs and promised that a guard will soon be stationed there. Local residents have been urged not to dump their garbage in the graveyard.

4. The following sentences contain statements of opinion or some other error. Rewrite each sentence so that there is no opinion or error.

   (a) Managers may find it worth their time to attend the Annual Lecture scheduled for March 15 at India International Centre.

   (b) The articulate young woman speaking with great confidence did not hesitate to tell the Editor that her news story was the best.

   (c) The famous furniture shop, established 50 years back, has scheduled an elaborate programme of several parties to celebrate its golden jubilee.

   (d) Another important theme at the annual authors meeting was the startling idea that it does not matter whether children begin to read before they are eight years old.

(e) The Municipal Corporation Delhi has announced that the citizens of the city can look forward to the construction of a New Town Hall at Ajmari Gate next year.

5. The following phrases have unnecessary words. You do not have to rewrite them. Just cross off the unnecessary words.

(a) true information. (b) red in colour. (c) fallen from higher to lower.
(d) shot to kill. (e) free presents (f) in order to.
(g) gone by history. (h) tracked down. (i) greatly different.
(j) youthful kid.

6. Rewrite the following sentences, correcting all their errors
   (a) He suffered the loss of his left hand.
   (b) He criticised the previous speaker and called him incoherent and goofy.
   (c) The Man-of the-Match expressed his thanks to those who had cheered him.
   (d) Before an adolescent boy reaches the age of 15, he will see a total of 10,000 scenes of violence on the TV.
   (e) The general agreement of opinion among the participating delegates was that it should be up to the chairman to finalise the resolution.
   (f) One of the negotiators brought out during the discussion that the terms of the contract would not be in accordance with the objectives of the company.
   (g) The 25-year-old young student, the son of a teacher, does not look serious but has become an expert on corporate law.
   (h) At a party given in his honour on the day of his retirement, the students of Modern School surprised the Principal by presenting him a car.
   (i) The Managing Director, his wife and their two children served as the perfect hosts at the annual dinner of the company.
   (j) Anil, a handsome young boy who is just 30-year old,

seems to be an unlikely person to write a book about the topic, yet his book about strategic marketing has become a best seller.

7. Cross out the unnecessary words
   (a) She was in a quick hurry and warned that, in the future, she will seek out textbooks that are vulgar and demand that they be totally banned.
   (b) As it now stands, three separate members of the committee said they would try to prevent the MCD from closing down the park during the summer months.
   (c) His car was totally destroyed and, in order to obtain the loan necessary to buy a new car, he now plans to apply to a bank for a loan to help him out.
   (d) After police found the dead body, the medical doctor conducted a post-mortem to determine the cause of death and concluded that the youth had been strangulated to death.
   (e) In the past, he often met up with the students at the computer lab and, because of their future potential, invited them to attend the convention.

8. Change the following long sentences into short sentences

   Clever lawyer that he was, Jinnah took the independence that Gandhi had wrestled for India from the British by rousing the masses to non-violent struggle and used it to set up his own independent but shaky Muslim nation to Pakistan, destined, I believed then, to break up, as shortly happened when the eastern Bengali part, separated from the western part by a thousand miles of India's territory, broke away to form Bangladesh, destined eventually, I believed, to simply disappear.

9. Try and make the following news story accurate.

   New Delhi: Seeking a rollback of all reservations based on caste by the government, members of Youth for Equality will march from Maulana Azad Medical College on Bahadur Shah Zafare Marg to Jantar Mantar on Wednesday. The protest march is expected to cause disruption of traffic in central Delhi and motorists are advised to avoid it.

The rally, which is scheduled to start at 2 p.m. from MAMC. Protesting medial students will march via Jawaharlal Nehru Marg, Ranjit flyover, Barakhamba Road, Tolstoy Marg, Sansad Marg to reach Jantar Mantar.

The march is expected to slow down movement of traffic at ITO, Delhi Gate, Tilak Marg, Sikandra Road, Vikas Marg, Subhash Marg, and Asaf Ali Marg. "Though it is being organised on a Saturday afternoon, it might lead to some congestion in the area," said a senior traffic police official.

ANSWERS

(1) Story reduced to 200 words

The corpse of three-month-old Kaku, son of Madhavpuram's Rahul Sharma, was missing from his grave after burial in Surajkund on Tuesday (11 a.m.). The family members found the grave dug up and body missing when they went there to perform some rituals in the night. Suspecting a *tantrik's* involvement they informed the police. However, people living in the neighbourhood blamed stray dogs and pigs.

A report in an evening newspaper hinted the involvement of a *tantrik* as bodies of at least 20 children were missing from their graves under suspicious circumstances. The police do not believe in this theory but said they would investigate the charge.

Local residents blame the authorities for allowing the graveyard to turn into a haunt for animals. "Dogs and pigs often dig out corpses from the graves," said Naresh. He said he had often had to scare away animals feeding on corpses. The Municipal Corporation looks after the burial ground.

Expressing grief over the incident Mayor has assured that the graveyard would be given a facelift. However, he held the district administration equally responsible for not raising the boundary wall to stop the entry of dogs and pigs. He promised to station a guard there.

Editing Prerequisites 55

(2) The Heading

The mystery of a missing infant's corpse

(3) The Lead

The corpse of an infant goes missing from city's cremation grounds.
Who is responsible—*tantrik* or stray animals?

(4) Rewritten with no opinion or error
   (a) The Annual Lecture is scheduled for March 15 at India International Centre.
   (b) The woman told the editor that her news story was the best.
   (c) The famous furniture shop has scheduled a dinner to celebrate its golden jubilee.
   (d) The annual authors meeting suggested that it does not matter whether children begin to read before they are eight year old.
   (e) The Municipal Corporation Delhi announced the construction of a New Town Hall at Ajmari Gate next year.

(5) Unnecessary words

	Delete	Use
(a) true information.	true	information
(b) red in colour.	in colour	red
(c) fallen from higher to lower.	From higher to lower	fallen
(d) shot to kill.	Shot to	kill
(e) free presents	free	presents
(f) in order to.	in order	to
(g) gone by history.	gone by	history
(h) tracked down.	down	tracked
(i) greatly different.	greatly	different
(j) youthful kid.	youthful	kid

(6) Sentences rewritten
(a) He lost his left hand.
(b) He called the previous speaker incoherent and goofy.
(c) The Man-of the-Match thanked his supporters.
(d) Before reaching 15, a young boy will watch 10,000 scenes of violence on TV.
(e) The participating delegates agreed that the chairman should finalise the resolution.
(f) The negotiators revealed that the terms of the contract were against the objectives of the company.
(g) The 25-year-old young student is an expert in corporate law.
(h) The students of Modern School gave a farewell party to the Principal and presented him a car.
(i) The Managing Director, his wife and their two sons served as perfect hosts.
(j) Anil's book on strategic marketing has become, a best seller.

(7) Cross the following words:
(a) quick; in the future; out; totally
(b) As it now stands; separate; down; months
(c) totally; in order; now; to help him out
(d) dead; medical; determine the cause of death; to death
(e) In the past; up with; future; attend

(8) Long sentences changed into short sentences

Jinnah, a clever lawyer, accepted independence that Gandhi had wrestled from the British. He used non-violent struggle to set up an independent shaky Muslim nation, Pakistan. It was destined to break up. It happened soon when the eastern Bengali part, separated from the western part by a thousand miles of India's territory, broke away to form Bangladesh.

(9) Inaccuracies in the news story

The story appeared on Saturday morning. It was a press release from the Delhi Police Traffic Department to inform the people about the likely obstructions to the traffic on certain roads. Therefore, the Wednesday cannot be correct. Also it clashes with Saturday in the last paragraph. Saturday seems to be the correct day. It seems the press release was dated Wednesday and therefore this confusion.

The second paragraph is confusing. The first sentence is incomplete. It should be edited in the following way:

The rally of protesting medial students, which is scheduled to start at 2 p.m. from MAMC, will march via Jawaharlal Nehru Marg, Ranjit flyover, Barakhamba Road, Tolstoy Marg, Sansad Marg to reach Jantar Mantar.

References:

Managing Editing, JohnMorrison, Routhledge.
Scoop: Inside Story from the Partition to the Present, Kuldip Nayar, Harper Collins.

4

Selecting News

Selecting news stories for the next day's edition is a usual and routine job of an editor. In fact, every evening a news meeting is held to decide what news is to be selected for the next day's edition. Equally important is the allocation of pages to the news. Important news is to be displayed on page one. Other news is allocated to the inside pages according to its importance. Along with that, a decision also has to be taken about the placement of the news item and the column spread to be given to it. Though it looks like a routine job, these are vital decisions and the editors have to use discretion and intelligence for selecting relevant news and deciding its page allocation, its placement on the page and the column spread it requires.

Debate on the guidelines of news selection has been going on since the day the first newspaper was launched. It is still continuing and would continue in the years that follow, without any definite agreement. It is and would remain to be a subjective process. All efforts to develop it into a science have not succeeded. It still is an art as no scientific tests or academic measurements have been developed to help editors judge a story's newsworthiness. The reason for this is that there is no widely acceptable definition of news. Therefore, it is not possible to arrive at factors affecting the selection of news.

Understanding News

Before we discuss how the desk editors should select news for the next edition, we must define what is meant by 'news', the word from which the newspaper derives its name. True, journalists have not been able to agree on what is news and do not have a universally acceptable definition of news. Nevertheless, we must try to know what the various views on the meaning of news are. This at least will enable us to have an understanding of what news is.

News is central to a newspaper or magazine. It is only when news arrives that editing begins. All those in the production process of a newspaper are concerned with giving readers information and ideas they have not heard before. Most of what appears in the newspaper, whether news stories or product reviews or gossip, is news. And most areas of content, work better when they are subjected to the discipline of news: topicality, relevance and accuracy. Therefore, all those working in the newspaper: reporters, correspondents, designers and desk editors, should understand what makes news for your publication.

Ideas about what makes news have been passed down over the years: When a 'dog bites a man' that is not news, but when a 'man bites a dog,' it is news. (The term is usually attributed either to John B. Bogart, City Editor or Charles A. Dana, editor of *New York Sun*.) The aphorism means that news should concern itself with the unexpected. The same has been said differently by Lord Northclife, the founder of *Daily Mail*, "News is anything out of the ordinary." Another adage is attributed to William Randolph Hearst, founder of the Hearst newspaper and magazine group in the USA, and to Northcliffe again: "News is what someone doesn't want you to print. Everything else is advertising." In other words, "news is that information that someone is hiding somewhere."

Dana gives a widely acceptable definition of news: "News is something which interests a large part of the community and has never been brought to their attention." This usually combines two important ideas. It reminds us that news is not something new, necessarily, but something your readers have not heard before.

> **Constituents of News**
>
> New: not known to your readers.
> Relevant: it has to affect them, be close to them or be made to seem so.
> Simple: or easily grasped.
> Finite: it should be an event, not a permanent condition.
> Surprising: any information that is amazing, astonishing and striking. It may be the most important quality of all.

News is not about information for its own sake. It is about information that is not known to readers. It need not be entertaining, in the narrow sense, but it should appeal to the readers and make them want to read on. This is the main difference between stories that appear on news pages and the raw handouts and press releases that are handed over to reporters to create news. The news becomes human-interest if it has an emotional impact. Dramatic action may be useful in making the news interesting. However, the dramatic part in the news has to be different for different types of readers. Dramatic events involving children and animals will be very useful on pages for children. It would not be suitable for women pages. A dramatic element in unexpected rulings in tax appeal would be appropriate for the business pages. In totality, the news has to be right for your readers.

Defining News

Much has been written and discussed on what we mean by 'news'. Academicians are in the habit of making concepts difficult to understand. For example Galtung and Ruge, two sociologists from Norway consider news as 'a crisis of variable intensity which is assessed by factors of personalisation or cultural proximity.' Not going into the intricacies of this, let us find a simpler definition of news. *Oxford Advanced Learner's Dictionary of Current English* defines news as, new or fresh information or reports of what has most recently happened. This means that events covering a wide range of descriptions involving people, animals and things, some marvellous, some mundane, becomes news merely through their existence being made known. An event that no one knows about—like the blinding of criminals in Bihar—was not public knowledge. It became so only when it was made known to the public many days later by newspapers. Therefore, news is any event or fact that has not been disclosed. Once disclosed it ceases to be news.

Keeping in view the above views on the meaning and nature of news, we can now determine the main characteristics of news. News should have the following characteristics:

01. There must be some focus in the news; either there should be a person who should be responsible for a certain incident or some happening that was unusual.

02. There should be some provocation in the whole incident; either there should be conflict, struggle, or development of some critical problem.

03. No situation can be news if it is not changing. There should be some action and state of affairs should be changing. Faster is the movement, the more important is the news.

04. There must be some impact on the people or community. For example, the murder of a child in a family may not be a news because murders in cities are every day happenings. But if the murder was committed by a domestic servant when the whole family was away it becomes news. It has an impact on the society. Families in cities leave their children behind with the servants and the children become their victims.

05. The entire incident should develop into an engaging scenario. For instance, the Aroshi murder case in NOIDA became an absorbing incident because the family reported that the murder was carried out by the domestic help. But the next day his body was found on the roof of the house. Later the police arrested the father and laid blame on so many other persons. The case, till mid 2009, was under investigation.

These five characteristics indicate that an event should have six essentials to qualify as news. They are:

Effect: News should affect, involve or interest the maximum number of readers.

Proximity: News should happen closer to the homes of readers. Besides physical closeness it may be psychological closeness also.

Conflict: News should have a factor of conflict to it. Clash could be between people, armies, nations or ideas.

Topical: News should be new, current and timely.

Celebrity: An event becomes newsworthy when distinguished and well-known persons are involved

Uniqueness: An incident becomes news if it is unique, unusual, far-fetched or strange.

Effect

No incident can be news if it does not create an impact on the people or the community. Stronger is the effect, the greater will be the news. A war affects a large number of persons and causes widespread damage to people, property and environment. It is always top news. Similarly any mass killings, riots or communal clashes in a city can cause turmoil in the society. This again will be important news. For example, the killing of a large number of children and women in Nithari village adjoining NOIDA in Utter Pradesh was one such news. When deciding whether or not to use the news, the editor should estimate how many and how deeply people would be affected. A higher priority should be given to news that may shock a large number of readers.

Desk editors should give top priority to news that affect, involve or interest the maximum number of readers. A terrorist attack that kills many persons is more important than a murder in the street because the former affects a large number of persons than the latter one.

Editing news of social and political impact is to be done in a very professional way and with great care. Such news affects a large number of readers and therefore any wrong information or analysis may have the most serious consequences. News that fall in this category should be edited precisely. Details need to be described in unambiguous terms—in clear, accessible and readable language.

An example:

> As the private bus operators went on strike in Delhi, the mass transit was paralysed for the second day. With negotiations failing, those dependent on public transport system, mostly belonging to the low income group of the society, felt economically harassed. Well-to-do citizens resorted to carpools while others took a taxi or three-wheeler scooter. Those who could not afford had to cover the distance walking. Those who could cancel shopping trips, errands, and even doctor's appointment if that were not urgently needed did so. Many employees, desperate to keep their jobs, said they would call in sick. Some had to walk for distances of 12 to 14 kilometres. "What else can I do?" asked poor Subhash Nath, 40, who said he had no other option but to set out before dawn from his house in Kirti Nagar to his restaurant job in Connaught Place to reach on time.

The desk-editor has been able to focus directly and intently on impact: thousands of commuters and their families suffered, particularly those belonging to the weaker sections. This, in fact, must have been felt by every *Delhiwalla*. The story has been edited to describe impact in real-life terms that any reader can understand: commuters must share cars or walk or cancel everyday activities. Giving personalised details, as of Subhash Nath, is much more effective than a simple generalised description that commuters were "greatly inconvenienced." Appropriate language and scenarios has been selected and used, to create proper impact. Efforts have been made to edit the story in human terms: Poor Subhash Nath, forced to set out before dawn to get to his restaurant job.

> "Wasting taxpayer funds" underlines the impact of the story below:
>
> Breaking from the norms of Delhi Municipal Corporation decorum, two councilors on Tuesday bashed each other for allegedly wasting taxpayer funds on buying luxury cars.
>
> Most of the newspaper readers pay taxes, directly or indirectly, so Delhi readers would read this story with enormous interest. Many may exclaim, "What? I pay taxes so those guys can buy expensive cars?"
>
> A great way to create an impact with your story.

Proximity

News becomes important if it happens closer to the homes of readers. Readers may not be interested in what is happening in far away places. A military coup in Fiji will be front-page news displayed in eight columns in that country. It might be given in the inside pages in the newspapers in Malaysia. But Indian newspapers would not give more than a paragraph of it and that too on an insignificant page. Local papers in Tamil Nadu or Kerala may not even include it in their news schedule as not many from those states are living in Fiji.

Likewise the wedding of a local political leader in Delhi will get a picture and half a column description in the Delhi edition of *The Hindustan Times* or *The Times of India* but will be completely ignored by their Kolkota or Mumbai editions.

Home, in fact, is more important than the other side of the globe. A joke in press clubs is that any event happening on the main street of the town—even two bulls fighting for nothing—is a bigger story than any other story. It would interest more readers than a major shake up or revolution in Africa or armed conflict between Russia and Chechnya separatists' forces. Jock Lauterer, an American professor correctly believes, "News is like a hurricane; the closer it gets, the more important it becomes to you".

> Suppose you have to select one news item from the following two news pieces:
>
> **Which one would you select for the Delhi edition if you are a citizen of Delhi?**
>
> A Maruti 800 hits a tree and all the occupants in the car die. The accident happens in Bhopal about 800 kilometres from Delhi.
>
> **Or**
>
> A single-engine plane crashes in the ridge in the backyard of Vasant Vihar in Delhi. The only occupant, the pilot, was killed.
>
> Obviously, you should select the plane-crash story and not the one about the car accident.
>
> The reason is that the plane crashed in the heart of your city and not in a far away place. The readers in Delhi would be more interested in reading the news and as much details about it as possible. It would also affect the readers of Delhi if the pilot were from Delhi.
>
> The readers of Delhi will be hardly interested in the car accident story.
>
> The car accident took place in a far away city and readers may not know the people involved in it.

Proximity is just not related to physical closeness alone. It may be psychological also. An efficient desk-editor will consider geographic and emotional closeness while selecting a story for the edition. One also feels closer because of other reasons like similarity of interests. People living thousands of miles away may share the same problem because of similarity of interest. The following news story is an example:

> As many as 10 teenagers in the small town of Bilaspur in Madhya Pradesh

are under investigation over counterfeit notes allegedly made by them using their personal computers. The boys were using the currency to buy garments in the local market, the police said.

The notes, mostly of five-hundred rupee denominations, looked real enough.

The person at the cash counter could not notice the difference. The notes were detected as fake only when the cashier went to the bank to deposit his daily sales proceeds yesterday.

Many routine stories on juvenile crimes would not cause widespread alarm. However, a story like this will concern most of the parents all over the country. This story is not only unusual but also shocking, and so would arouse national interest. Many readers would be having school-going children. Therefore, children counterfeiting money and spending in the busy market even in a small town will cause worry to them. Parents of school-going children in Delhi or Mumbai will sympathise with the parents of the 10 teenagers in Bilaspur. Therefore, the story will be read with concern and interest.

Proximity should be defined liberally because something happening on the other side of the globe can be of interest in India too. Suppose the story is about the development of a new cure for diabetes—a pharmaceutical company has developed an oral pill to substitute insulin injection. This news will be of major interest all over the country as diabetes is a wide-spread disease in India and hundreds of thousands of people may be on injections. They will all be relieved if this pill were to be made available in India. Therefore, readers in India will be interested in finding out more about the pill. The news would have the closeness element though the news is from the other side of the globe.

Every newspaper has space constraints. It has to set a few parameters for deciding what to publish and what not to. The nearness or geographical factor in such a situation becomes an important element in the selection of news.

Conflict

Any clash makes news. It can be between people, armies, nations or ideas. Two persons fighting on a busy street even though on a petty issue is more newsworthy than two persons agreeing to solve their conflict peacefully. Any clash that takes place causes tension in the area and that makes the story dramatic and interesting to read. Many, particularly those in the government and the corporate sector, consider controversial stories on policies and problems as negative news. But such stories cannot be ignored because they provide readers with different opinions about policies and problems. These stories also help readers in understanding issues and to find solutions that may check conflicts in the future. If the issue of the West Bengal Government taking over the land from the farmers in Singur and Nandigram villages were debated in the media, the intense conflict that led to much blood spilling could have been restrained. However, to edit conflict stories carefully and colourfully but calmly is the professional responsibility of every editor.

Example:

The following story is an example of a conflict that is often in the news. The following story is significant from the editing viewpoint because it shows the superficial and obvious news element, as well as a deeper story behind the conflict.

> Harare, Zimbabwe: Riots sparked by rising food prices spread on Tuesday as crowds stoned cars, trashed suburban shops and marched through the streets. Police fired tear gas in response and soldiers patrolled the poorest neighbourhoods.
>
> With Zimbabwe's economy in tatters, the government last week announced increases of up to 30 per cent on bread, sugar and soft drink prices. Bus and taxi-van fares rose on Monday. The new higher prices followed a series of increases in the cost of gasoline, milk, and corn meal—a staple food.

The superficial news in the above story is riots. The deeper and more important issue that the story reveals is the impact of economic hardship on the law and order situation of the country. The deteriorating economy of Zimbabwe has hurt its people so much that they have taken to the streets without caring for their lives. They think if they must die they better die fighting.

A conflict is always news because it can escalate into violence; at times into a serious fury that can have a widespread affect if not properly handled. The removal of Dr. B. R. Ambadekar's statue in Lucknow (Uttar Pradesh) caused serious violence in many parts of India. Blood, agony and tears alone are not news; more often, what is behind the story is the real news.

The story below gets directly to the deeper meaning of conflict:

> A slow development of opposition to the city's master plan for building on the Yamuna waterfront is gaining strength, threatening to delay construction of the first major project before the 2010 Commonwealth Game.
>
> Activities in the neighbourhood far removed from the 1,000-acre commercial plan—where officials want to construct a mini-city of hotels, a housing complex and office towers—are holding drawing room meetings, organising petition drives, and planning public rallies to find a way for the withdrawal of the plan.
>
> "People are furious," said Subhash Nath of the Federation of RWA's that has been receiving calls from residents of housing societies in the surrounding areas. "People are suddenly realising what's being planned over there and they're not happy."
>
> The uprising has alarmed the authorities, which believed until recently that the plan was due for approval by the Ministry of Environment.

In the above story you will find five factors that a conflict story which has been selected and edited for publication in a newspaper must have:

1. *Characterise the conflict.* In this case it is a non-violent, slow opposition to the master plan for the waterfront area.

2. *Isolate the deeper meaning.* It is the opposition to the master plan.
3. *How the conflict is manifested is to be made prominent in the story.* The drawing room meetings and petition drives are the manifestations.
4. *Quote participants.* See how the story has been made more effective by quoting a person—"People are furious," rather than merely saying, "people are angry".
5. *Show the effect of the clash.* You do it by saying that the city authorities were alarmed.

Desk-editors should not fall into the habit of converting every conflict, even non-violent confrontation, into warlike situations. The story below shows how teachers are being characterised as 'fighting' in what really is a non-violent dispute over their pay:

> While teachers in the government schools celebrate heafty pay raises, teachers in non-aided schools are fighting to get what they say is their right to get a parity in pay with teachers in government schools.
>
> Officials from the Director of Education's office have been asked to settle disputes in the capital as negotiations between teachers' union and school authorities have failed.

When editing clash stories the desk-editor should be very careful about two points. *Firstly*, every situation should not be painted grim. Do not follow the dictum that 'noise and smoke are always news'. Try to find out the deeper meaning—the reason for the clash—and you will find the real news for your reader.

Secondly, you should be careful about the language. Writing that politicians are 'attacking' each other and school teachers 'fighting' may take your story beyond its intrinsic newsworthiness and mislead your readers.

Topical

Only what is new, current and timely is news. Newspapers all over the world are designed to provide current information.

They compete with each other to break the news first and report it much before their rivals do so. An event that took place a week or fortnight back is of no relevance to newsreaders. If such news were to be included, the desk-editor would insist on fresh and additional information on which the story could be developed and may look current. Sometimes a story needs a background to make the readers understand the news in the right perspective. If it is essential to give the background, do not allocate it much space in the story. It should be woven throughout the story in such a way that it becomes a part of it.

The senior editors in a newspaper always tell new desk-editors that readers are not interested in knowing historical facts and details, though these might be interesting. A popular advice is that readers do not want to read how the earth was formed billions of years ago despite the description being fascinating and interesting. They also are not much interested in reading that billions of years from now because of climatic changes the earth may either freeze or burn up. People do not wait anxiously for the newspapers in the morning to read such type of news and writings.

A professional desk-editor is trained to stay on the cutting edge of daily events. He must watch the people who would make news in the edition the next day. They must read between the lines and look for hidden meanings, and try to understand what would be the likely course of events in the next few days. It requires total engrossment in current events, reading as many newspapers and magazines as possible and watching news on different news channels.

The primary responsibility of an editor in the intensely competitive world of newspapers and television is to come up with scoops and exclusive news pieces. It is the most basic and perhaps the most important form of editing.

An example:

> A Delhi police officer was run over by a speeding car last night while he and his assistant were at the check post in the Connaught Place area.

Selecting News

No doubt, your readers want reporting and analyses of the compelling economic, political and social happenings and issues of the day, but first they also want to read "what was all that fuss over in Connaught Place last night".

While trying to be timely, you should always keep two things in mind. First, competing to be the first does not mean sloppy and inaccurate editing. You should be the first, if you can, but you must always be accurate. The drive for timeliness should not override your need to be careful, thoughtful and accurate.

Second, old news is news for your readers if they do not know it yet. Do not get so overpowered by timeliness that you automatically discard news unless it broke within the past 24 hours. If you have missed a story, your challenge is to present it in a new perspective. A story can always be rewritten in more than one way to illustrate the topicality and meaning for readers, even if the development took place days, or weeks or months ago. For example the news of the blinding of a group of hard criminals in Bhagalpur jail, known as 'Bhagalpur Blinding' on which the movie, *Gangajal* was based was first reported by a regional newspaper. The national dailies came to know of it much later. But they had to report it to their readers. They rewrote the news to make it current and raised questions about the police and human rights. It became an issue of public debate.

Celebrity

If you have been reading newspapers regularly you might have observed that news stories normally cover people who are celebrities. An event becomes newsworthy when distinguished and well-known persons (now also known as 'Page 3' persons) are involved. If anything happens to the common man, no one takes any notice, even if it is a serious incident. But when the same thing happens to the stars, the affluent and illustrious it becomes news. Several car accidents happen on the roads in Mumbai. Not many are in the news. But when Salman Khan was involved in an accident it became major front-page news. There was a joke that when Indira Gandhi sneezed it was news, while the sneeze in itself is not newsworthy since thousands do it every minute. No doubt then that Page 3 is the most widely read section of every newspaper. Its pages are filled up with information and pictures about the lives and activities of the glamourous, celebrated and powerful people. So, the priority in selecting a story for editing should be determined by the following question: Is this person or happening of compelling interest to the readers?

But it is not the universal principle that only prominent persons and places should be selected for the edition. Even an unknown person without any power or wealth can make news if they accomplish something unusual or if something extraordinary happens to them. This can be illustrated with the help of two stories where the prominence factor has been edited differently.

The following story gets selected because Medha Pathkar is a 'prominent environmental activist' who is known to millions of people not only in India but the world over. Her arrest will make news. Also her name must appear in the first paragraph because mentioning it in the second paragraph would not focus properly on the prominence factor which is so important in news editing.

Example:

> Tehri Garhwal: The police on Sunday arrested environmentalists, including a prominent activist Medha Pathkar, during a protest march at the closing of the last tunnel in Tehri.

> In this other story, the boy is not as important as what he is but he is an unfortunate victim of the volatility of war. His death was watched on television worldwide. The story is a good one despite the fact it happened in place that may not be known to a large number of readers in India. But it is a good human-interest story that would emotionally affect every one.

> Bureiji Refugee Camp, Gaza Strip: He died huddled in his father's arms, caught in a hail of bullets, captured in the

viewfinder of a television camera in a shocking scene viewed all over the world.

Twelve-year old Mohammed Jamal Aldura—was shot as his desperate father tried to shield him after they blundered into the middle of a fierce Israeli-Palestinian clash outside a small Jewish settlement—was mourned yesterday in the teeming refugee camp where he spent his short life...

An Associated Press story has become a classic example where the person was not important at all but the international reaction on his capital punishment made him newsworthy. The unknown Miguel got prominence in the news only because international activists against capital punishment came to his aid, to no avail.

Huntsville, Texas: A Mexican-born killer was executed by injection Thursday amid protests from countries that say he was denied his right under an international treaty to contact the Mexican consulate after his arrest.

About five hours before Miguel Flores was strapped to a gurney for the execution, the U.S. Supreme Court, in a 5–4 vote, denied his request for a reprieve...

The prominence factor, however, does not give freedom to the journalists to chase well-known persons in their private as well as public moments, to serve nothing more exalted than the base instincts of people who like to peer into other people's bedrooms.

Prominence is not confined only to people. Ideas, issues, things—all can fit in the definition of prominence, and the editing priorities should be adjusted accordingly.

A few examples:

1. Graffiti on a subway wall in the city is not news; graffiti defacing the South Block building is.
2. Demonstrations against pollution are relatively minor news; demonstrations against racial, gender and ethnic discrimination are big news.
3. Taxes, health care, education and crime are news because they affect every Indian citizen.

Uniqueness

A story can be news if it captures the readers' attention because it seems so unique and unusual, far-fetched or strange. Some stories are news simply because they are so unusual; such radical departures from the expected, that they fascinate many readers. For example, an incident like the following:

> A ten-year old boy was in critical condition and his father unhurt after their car collided into another car.
>
> The accident occurred on Jan Path in New Delhi as the father, his wife and son were coming home after attending a family lunch. While driving at a normal speed of 50 kilometre an hour, the car hit another stationary car parked on the road.
>
> The boy was sitting in the front passenger seat, the side that hit the stationary car. Since his wife was sitting in the rear seat she was unhurt. The father was also unhurt as the right side of the car had no impact of collision.

The story is news simply because it is tragic, even if it has no meaning (than, perhaps, that life is fickle). The story will interest readers because it is odd.

These are the six factors that should be kept in mind while selecting stories for the edition. Though these factors are significant in the selection process, they work on a sliding scale. The geographical factor is not absolute. International news would get a higher priority if it affects the national interests of the country. For example, purchase of military hardware by Pakistan in the United States will definitely get front page selection in any national daily in India. Sliding scale works equally with the celebrity factor. A speech at the election rally in Lucknow might not be covered by a national daily like *The Statesman* but it would get a prominent display in *The Hindustan Times* published from that city.

News is defined as the first disclosure of a fact or an event; there is no absolute scale of value by which it stands to be selected for publication for the edition of the day. For the purpose of selecting news for your paper you should take into account all these six factors and then qualify them, relating them to the special interests of the paper and its readers. A business paper should give priority to news concerning technology, energy and economic development. A financial paper should select news that is related to stock markets, banks and financial institutions. The popular tabloids should give precedence to human-interest stories.

News selection is a very subjective process and the newspapers have failed to apply objective criterion. It is because of the absence of absoluteness in news assessment that newspapers display such diversity of content, though all would be giving prominence to stories of fundamental importance.

5

Editing the Main Story

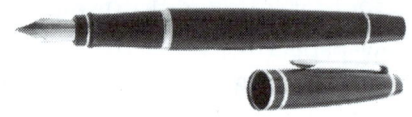

Editing is an essential skill that every journalist should possess, especially one who wants to be successful in his profession and desires to reach the top. Editing is the art of reshaping a story to attract readers. It does not involve giving a literary flair to a news story; rather it is the process of giving a shape and size to the story so that readers find it interesting and informative while reading. This, in fact, is also the first principle of editing. Editing is an art that can be acquired through learning and practice.

A desk-editor has to ensure that the news story is edited with a narrative drive and an economy of words. It should be understandable to the readers in the shortest possible time spent by them. Like the design of news pages, editing also is needed for functional reasons. The purpose is to grab the immediate attention of the readers, give them the key points as quickly as possible and provide the remaining information in the order of importance. In other words, the story should be constructed in such a way that the reader does not pause and feel disconcerted. The vocabulary should be simple so that understanding and comprehension is quick and easy. Good editing will give the readers the essence of the news right in the beginning, and unfold the details of the story in a logical and interesting way. The story should be balanced and the contents of the story fair and accurate.

News Editing is Technical

Editing news stories is a specialised job. It is different from editing books or other types of writings like academic, corporate or official. Academic writing is done by scholars, researchers and academicians of high caliber. Their writings are knowledge-based and language-oriented. These are written after intensive research, reading books and journals, and consulting factual material on the net. The academicians write with a certain opinion and hypothesis which they try to prove or disprove. So the approach is analytical. They prove their point or dismiss other views by giving lots of quotations, footnotes and references. Such writings are followed by a large bibliography. The entire effort is to show how much the academician has read on the subject. It follows an 'introduction-thesis-body-conclusion' formula.

Corporate writing is market-oriented, which is formal and legal. It is 'to-the-point' and tries to commit the other party to certain things to benefit the main party.

Official or bureaucratic writing is non-committal. It is written in a style that makes the person or the department not responsible for actions being done or is to be done.

Writing news stories differs from the above three writings in many ways.

First, a news reporter collects information mainly from talking or listening to people. Collection of material from books or magazines is minimal. Official documents connected with the news may have to be read and consulted but these are mentioned to prove the point and not as reference.

Secondly, the quotations are merged in the body of the news story. These are not cited as footnotes or reference lists. Quotations are not given simply to show how well read a peron is, but these are attributed to persons to give authenticity to the news.

Thirdly, the writing is organised to give information to the readers. It is given according to its importance to them and not to prove or disprove a thesis. It is a candid collection of facts and information that should bring alive the incident that has happened. Each story should develop an imagery so that the reader may feel that he was present at the scene of the event.

Editing a News Story

It is not difficult to write a news story. "It is easy. All you have to do is sit down at a typewriter and open a vein," says New York Times' sportswriter, Red Smith. But the task of editing a news story is more difficult, though challenging and interesting. The desk-editor has to check the story as submitted by the reporter and okay it before sending it for page making. He has to correct all errors, be it in grammar, spelling, or usage and see that the writing style of the newspaper is followed. Also important is the fact that all stories are well structured, quotes are properly used and issues and events are properly placed, besides ensuring that the approved writing style of the newspaper is meticulously followed.

A news story has three parts—headline, lead and the main story or body. The headline is the main heading that breaks the news and attracts the reader to go through the story. The lead is the first paragraph of the story that gives the most newsworthy information. It also reveals the central point of the story with the objective of arousing further interest of the reader in the story. The section of the story that follows the lead and develops it into a full story is called the 'main story' or the body of the story. It contains information that the reader must know.

Editing the Main Story

Editing the main or the body of the story is the most arduous job because the report filed by the reporters and correspondents may not be organized in the fashion in which the story will be published in the columns of the newspaper. The newspapers put in special efforts to make the story readable, easy-to-follow and interesting. This job is done by the editing desk that consists of sub-editors and copy editors. This is a specialised job for which certain skills are required, which should be developed through academic exercises. A lot of thinking, research and discussions have taken place in the United States of America and Britain that has led to the development of different techniques for editing different types of stories—news-oriented, narrative, human interest, opinionated and so on. Unfortunately, the Indian university system has not been able to develop academics of journalism. Therefore, we have to take the theoretical structure of techniques developed by researchers in the US and Britain. These techniques are being followed, though inadvertently. However, a systematic editing training to teach these techniques has not been followed. We have found four approved styles useful for editing main bodies of news stories. These are:

1) Inverted pyramid
2) Hourglass
3) Focus
4) Narrative

Inverted Pyramid Style

This is the most popular and the oldest style of news editing. All over the world journalists follow this technique in writing or editing their stories. In this technique, every paragraph unfolds more information to take the story to its final form. These paragraphs contain information about the persons related with the news and their identifications, their views and quotes, explanation given by the authorities and any other information that goes to make the story unique, interesting and worth reading. Mitchell Stephens, who did in-depth research on the history of news, is of the view that the "inverted pyramid organizes stories not around ideas or chronologies but around facts. It weighs and shuffles the various pieces of information focusing with remarkable single-mindedness on their relative news value".

Importance is the dominant organising principle in this technique. News is arranged according to its relative importance. The story should commence with the most important, current or interesting information or news.

Information that is appealing and interesting and which is likely to attract the readers' attention should be given first priority. It should, in fact, reveal the news focus or the news in a nutshell and should be described in the first paragraph.

The second paragraph should describe the importance of the story. It may be called the 'key or core paragraph' because it explains why the story is important. In the American phraseology it is known as the 'nut graph'. After the core paragraph, the background or other relevant information should be given. The rest of the story should contain other information. All paragraphs should be arranged in the diminishing order of importance; earlier paragraphs should contain more important information and the less important news should be in the latter ones.

This technique is probably as old as the newspapers themselves. However, the technique was widely used during the Civil War in the United States. According to Stephens, telegraph, in those times, was the only means available to the reporters to transmit their stories from the battlefront. Many a time, the reports filed did not reach in full and the latter portions of the news were either unreadable or deleted. The reporters did not want that the relevant and important information get left out when their reports were published, and so they followed the most logical method of writing—reporting the most important information first.

This style is labeled as the 'inverted pyramid' because the top of the story is heavy, information-filled and loaded with facts.

Using the Inverted Pyramid Style

It basically is a style of writing that should be followed when writing a story, but one which reporters invariably find difficult to follow. The reason is that when a reporter is filing his story he is running against time. As the deadline has to be met, he writes his story without following any order of priority. The story ends up without any priority to events, facts and information. Therefore, their report may contain less important information in the beginning and the most important information at the end. It is the desk-editor who has to edit the story so that the reader does not miss out on important information. Therefore, every desk-editor must learn the inverted pyramid technique. Let us see how we can use this style to write a story.

Arrange the story

The first essential step is to organise the story. Let us take a train accident story. The inverted pyramid technique can best be explained with the help of such a story. It covers many aspects of news and helps in describing how news can be arranged according to its relative importance. Also a train accident affects a large number of people from different parts of the country. Friends and relatives are always concerned for their people in the train that has met with an accident.

Example:

We give here a story of a train accident that happened in April 2005.

The first paragraph is the lead that gives the focus of the news—the accident and number of persons killed and injured. It straightaway provides the main information about the accident. It also identifies the train and gives the location of the accident.

An accident is a human interest story also. Therefore, the first thing readers would like to know is the harm to human lives. So the maximum details i.e., the loss of lives and the number of injured are given in the second paragraph after the lead. Damage to the train is secondary and is described later in paragraph four.

The next important aspect is the accident. Paragraph three describes the exact location of the accident. This information is important because readers who are interested in knowing about the welfare of their people can call up friends and relatives in that area and ask them to enquire about them.

Then the readers would be interested in knowing the severity of the accident and the extent of damage to the train so that the enormity of the accident can be assessed. Paragraph four describes the number of coaches involved and the proportion of damage to them.

Paragraph five and six are almost of equal importance. Both describe how the rescue operations were being conducted. In an accident, the relief provided to the sufferers depends on the speed and efficiency of rescue operations. The two paragraphs describe in detail how the affected persons were being shifted to hospitals. The name of the hospital is also mentioned so that the people can find their relatives and friends and take care of them.

Paragraph seven describes in detail the accident itself and the reasons that caused it. It shows that the reporter went into minor details and gave a graphic version of how the system was not operated by the railway staff.

Paragraph eight mentions information collected from the surviving guard of the goods train. The quotation of the guard adds detail as well as a pleasing change of pace. Probably the reporter did not have much time to talk to the passengers, railway officials, the police, persons in the neighbourhood who immediately reached the site of the accident and helped rescue the passengers, and others who were present at the site of the accident. Speaking to them would have added a personal touch to the story. Probably the reporter had to meet the deadline and did not get enough time to collect this information.

Paragraph nine is a routine announcement that is of no interest to the readers. So also is paragraph ten. It politicises the accident and shows the politicians in poor light. These two paragraphs are of less importance and are not essential to the story. These two can be deleted if space is limited. The significance of the story would still be maintained even if the last two paragraphs were removed.

This, however, cannot be a standard style and organisation of a story edited in inverted pyramid style. Every story is different and even if it is not, it should be made so. The exact organisation of a story will depend on the facts and the newsworthiness of the story. Nevertheless, the first three

Editing the Main Story

paragraphs after the lead (2nd to 4th paragraphs) should always provide the most important details about the news and these should support and develop the lead.

Let us now read the story as it appeared:

1. Lead: Sabarmati Express collided with stationary goods train killing 17 and injuring 127, near Vadodra, Gujarat.

2. 17 people (including the driver of the Sabarmati Express and his assistant) were killed and over 127 injured (10 are in critical condition) when the Ahmedabad bound passenger train from Varanasi, (Train No. 9168 Sabarmati Express), collided with a stationary goods train (on the same track!) near Samlaya village in Vadodara district of Gujarat state at around 0310 Hrs (IST) on Thursday, 21 April 2005. The goods train was on the same track on which Shabarmati Express was running.

3. The train had departed Varanasi on Tuesday, 19 April afternoon at 1345 Hrs and was only three hours away from its destination, Ahmedabad. Samlaya is 43 kms from Godhra which was the last stop of the ill-fated train. Vadodara, which was to be the next stop, is just a distance of 30 kms. Scheduled arrival time at Ahmedabad, that was 130 kms away, was 0620 Hrs.

4. In all, seven coaches were damaged due to the mishap including three bogies of the goods train. The damaged coaches of Sabarmati Express were mangled and the engine and two passenger coaches had jumped track and were on top of the goods train. The early morning hour and the darkness hampered the relief work in the beginning, but the railway police and the fire brigade soon took over.

5. Rescuers used gas cutters and drilling tools to access the badly damaged coaches to rescue the survivors and retrieve the dead. Senior Railway officials inspecting the accident site said the number of casualties was less because the engine had taken the maximum brunt of the collision and was tossed on top of the goods train bogey. They cut open the mangled remains of the bogies to look for survivors and bodies inside.

Eight ambulances were dispatched to the accident site and the injured were rushed to SSG Hospital, Vadodara.

6. A disaster management team was rushed from Gandhinagar. The Gujarat administration immediately swung into action, with four ministers being sent to the accident site to co-ordinate relief operations.

7. The Sabarmati Express would not have met this fatal accident had the signal maintainer or the points man at 'B' cabin informed the station superintendent at Samlaya that the automatic signalling system had failed. Had the superintendent known, he could have informed the Ahmedabad-bound passenger train to slow down and the tragedy could have been averted.

Along with the 'human error', railway officials point to a mechanical failure of a bell crank lever—popularly known as the point—on the track. A point enables a train to shift tracks.

Railway officials believe that the pointsman tried to normalise the point manually.

In circumstances where the automatic signalling system fails, the driver is asked to slow the train to a minimum speed and the signal maintainer clears the train from that malfunctioning zone by walking in front of the engine with a green flag, a procedure which was not followed, say railway officials. However, following the signal failure, the point did not revert to its original position and took the Sabarmati Express into the loop line and Sabarmati Express rammed into the stationary goods train

8. One of the survivors of this terrible tragedy was the guard of the goods train, Pyarelal Mina, who escaped with few injuries. According to Mina, "the goods train arrived in Samlaya at 0230 hrs in the morning after which it stayed stationary on the loop track. The Sabarmati was expected on the main track but it came on the loop track, the result of which was the fatal accident." Mina recalls that the tail lights of the goods train was on so it would have been spotted by the crew of the oncoming train.

Editing the Main Story 85

9. The Railway Minister announced an ex-gratia of Rs One Lakh to the next of kin of those killed and an assistance of Rs 15,000 to the injured. Apart from the ex-gratia amount, the Railways would also provide employment to a member of the family of each of the deceased, Lalu Prasad told reporters at Vadodara airport.

10. The Railway Minister visited the accident site and later went to see the injured in Vadodara hospital where he faced angry demonstrations by suspected Bajrang Dal activists who stoned his car. Bajrang Dal is an affiliate of the state ruling political party, Bharatiya Janata Party (BJP). The Railway Minister accused Gujarat Chief Minister of orchestrating the attack to "kill" him. The minister was targeted as the accident was reportedly caused by error of the railway staff.

This unfortunately has given a political twist to the tragedy. Lalu Prasad Yadav's political party, the Rashtriya Janata Dal (RJD), stalled the Lok Sabha (Lower House of the Indian Parliament) proceedings demanding dismissal of the Gujarat government and implementation of the President's Rule in Gujarat. The Parliament was adjourned till Monday, 25th April.

Important Aspects of the Inverted Pyramid Style

When the technique of inverted pyramid style is being used to edit a story, certain points need to be kept in mind. Here are a few:

THE SECOND PARAGRAPH

The second paragraph is in fact the beginning of the story and is as important as the lead itself. Therefore, it is as difficult to write as the lead itself. The effective way to write it would be to clearly identify the news in the first sentence. It, however, should not be the repetition of the lead. It should be written differently and should provide a smooth and logical transition from the lead to the succeeding paragraphs.

The reporters normally fail to clearly mention the main news in the first two paragraphs. If a desk-editor allowed the story to go like that, the story would be vague, dull and disorganised. The main job of the editor, therefore, would be to see that this insufficiency is removed and only a clearly written second paragraph, highlighting the news goes in the print.

MAINTAIN A SEQUENCE

A story should unfold in a natural way and the main persons in the news should be identified in the first paragraph. Reporters often commit a common mistake of not mentioning the main person in the news while writing the first paragraph. However, they start the second paragraph with a name of a person they wanted to mention in the lead. They fail to make it clear that the person referred to in the second paragraph is the same one who was mentioned in the lead. Readers have to make a guess and many may be confused because the name is dropped suddenly. This is a common problem seen in the reporters' copy. This phenomenon is known as 'leapfrogging' in the American parlance. It can be avoided by giving a one- or two-word transition from the lead to the name in the second paragraph.

An Example

Reporter's Copy: A 55-year-old-man wept today after the City Magistrate found him innocent of theft.

Om Prakash was arrested six months ago.

Edited: A 55-year-old man wept today after a City Magistrate found him innocent of theft.

The defendant, Om Prakash, was arrested six months back.

Avoid deviation

After a smooth transition from the lead to the second paragraph, the effort should be to continue with the information that has been summarised in the lead. Many reports do not follow this rule. They fail to continue with the focus of the news after the second paragraph. They shift to a different topic reaching the third and subsequent paragraphs. This makes the story confusing and it becomes difficult to comprehend it.

Example:

> *Reporter's Copy:* New Delhi (4 October): The city police spend more of their time in attending to family disputes than to any other type of fights.
>
> A. P. Garg has been the West Delhi DCP for more than one year. He has seen many murders and much crime, but he says he never wanted to shift to any other profession.
>
> *Edited:* New Delhi (4 October): The city police spend more of their time attending to family disputes than to any other type of fights.
>
> West Delhi DCP, A. P. Garg, has been in this district for more than a year. Though he hates such calls because complainants get angry and irrational, and some take their anger out on police, he does not want to shift to any other profession.

The reporter's copy discussed two different issues. The lead summarised a problem that confronted most of the police officers in Delhi: Getting calls to settle family disputes. The second paragraph shifted to the DCP's career goals. It failed even to mention the problem of family disputes. The desk-editor eliminated this deviation by mentioning that though the police officers do not want to receive calls to settle family disputes, they do not want to change their profession.

Several names

A reporter while collecting information on a news story gets in touch with a number of people. He is always interested in including all the names and their identities in his report. This gives more importance to the persons than to the news. In fact, emphasis should be on the news and not on persons. Undue importance to names should be avoided and emphasis should be on the incident. The name or identity of relevant person or persons is necessary but not of all those who gave information. What various persons said, saw or did is to be included in the report and not who they are. Here is an example:

> *Reporter's Copy:* A mason was killed yesterday morning when a running bull hit the scaffolding of a balcony in Green Park area.

The mason, Ram Pal of R. K. Construction, was killed in the mishap while he was being transported to the hospital.

Puneet Lal, a carpenter from Rampur, reported the accident to the police.

Edited: The scaffolding for a balcony to a new apartment building collapsed, killing a mason working in the Green Park area.

A running bull hit the scaffolding that fell on mason Ram Pal. He died on way to the hospital.

Puneet Lal, a carpenter on the site, said he tried to warn the mason when the bull was charging towards the scaffolding. But Ram Pal could not hear it because of the noise caused by the construction work.

Advantages

The inverted pyramid style has a few advantages over other newly developed techniques of editing. Stories edited in the inverted pyramid style would satisfy the majority of the readers. The reason is that most of the newspaper readers are in a great hurry in the morning. They want to know the all-important news of the day in the shortest possible time. Therefore, most of them do not read the full story. They read only the first few paragraphs of the story because they just want to know all the important facts and information about the incident. Secondly, the inverted pyramid style helps the editor when he is making the page. It enables the editors to cut the story to any size if space is a problem. Stories can be chopped from the bottom without losing important facts and information.

Disadvantages

Many editors are not in favour of this style of editing. All stories become similar in style when this technique is used frequently, particularly in the same edition. This becomes dull and monotonous and reading the newspaper becomes uninteresting.

Secondly, the reader does not remain interested in the story throughout. The lead gives the central point and the second paragraph reveals the whole news. Nothing is left in the story for the reader to continue reading. Therefore, the story becomes irrelevant after the second paragraph because the reader does not read it beyond the second paragraph.

Thirdly, this style is not suitable for contemporary newspapers. In the present day lifestyle, the television news channels give continuous coverage of all the news as it keeps unfolding during the day. So the lead and the news is no more a surprise for the newspaper reader. In fact, he wants to know more details that were missed by the television.

Lastly, the style is stereotyped and does not need any expertise to edit a story. Editing becomes mechanical and routine because an editor is not able to show his special talents. Editing becomes formula-based and the editor cannot show his unique style of writing.

Nevertheless, it remains the most common form of editing because it is convenient to the editor when he is arranging the page. Moreover, deadline pressures encourage its use. A new style needs more time for writing.

Hourglass Style

Many editors do not prefer to use the inverted pyramid style because they do not find it a natural one. News according to them should be reported as it unfolds, not in a stereotyped way. They also feel that if only the inverted pyramid style is followed, all stories would look alike. They may be correct because all the stories cannot be narrated in exactly the same way. Stories on the skyrocketing or plunging Sensex, on the serial killer in Mumbai and the killing of more than 40 children in Nithari in NOIDA cannot be narrated the same way. Some stories, as the killing of children in a house in Nithari in NOIDA, need to be told following the chronological style. Such stories generally focus on a sequence of events that unfold in a dramatic or interesting way. A narrative style is needed to develop and write these stories. The style that combines the inverted pyramid and the narrative format was introduced in editing by Roy Peter Clark of *St. Petersburg (Fla.) Times.*

The technique follows the inverted pyramid style in the beginning. The beginning paragraphs reveal the most important information about the news. At the most, the first three to five paragraphs are used to describe all the important information about the news. The story should be developed in detail in these paragraphs. The storytelling method and narration of chronology is to be used while editing the story so that readers can understand how the whole incident happened.

After describing the news in detail a turn or twist should be introduced in the story. Great care has to be taken at this time because the story must become interesting at this point. This is the key to success of the hourglass style as it is at this point where you change from information to narration. Quotations, details and anecdotes can be added here.

This style is useful in stories about crime, accidents, changing weather conditions, natural disasters, election campaigns, sports, games and matches. In such stories information is to be given in sequence, while twists and turns are also possible. It, however, should not be used for those stories that do not have a meaningful chronological order like public meetings, cabinet meetings or Board meetings. In such meetings topics are not discussed in any logical order and a chronology is difficult to follow.

Example:

1. In a landmark judgment, the Supreme Court on Wednesday upheld Parliament's decision to expel 11 MPs for their involvement in the December 2005 cash-for-query scam. The court also upheld the expulsion for another Rajya Sabha member whose petition it heard alongside. The court described the expulsions as a 'self-protection' exercise by Parliament.

2. The judgment put to rest apprehensions of a confrontation between the judiciary and the legislature when the presiding officers of the Lok Sabha and the Rajya Sabha had refused to accept the court's notices on the petitions moved by the expelled members.

3. A five-judge Constitution bench headed by the Chief Justice Y. K. Sabharwal held by 4 to 1 majority that Parliament has the power to expel erring MPs.

4. However, the Court refused to accept that Parliament's actions were not subject to judicial review. "Proceedings which may be tainted on account of substantive or gross illegality or unconstitutionality are not protected from judicial scrutiny," the bench said. The court rejected the Centre's argument that the exercise of parliamentary privileges under Article 105 could not be circumscribed by other constitutional provisions such as the fundamental rights enshrined. It said the court cannot be "prevented from scrutinising the validity of the action of the legislature trespassing on the fundamental rights conferred on citizens".

5. It clarified, however, that judicial review did not mean that the jurisdiction of the legislature was being usurped by the court.

6. The court said that the "truth or correctness of the material (relied upon by the legislature for taking action) will not be questioned by the court nor will it go into the adequacy of the material or substitute its opinion for that of the legislature".

7. The ruling clears confusion over the extent and scope of uncodified parliamentary privileges under Article 105 (Parliament) and 194 (state assemblies) on which the opinion of the high courts has been divided.

8. Terming the judgement as "momentous", noted constitutional expert, Fali S. Nariman said the Supreme Court showed "great judicial statesmanship".

9. In the cash-for-query scam, sting operation by a private TV channel had shown the MPs accepting money for raising questions in Parliament. Ten of them from the Lok Sabha: Annasaheb M. K. Patil, Y. G. Mahajan, Pradeep Gandhi, Suresh Chandel and C. P. Singh (all from BJP), N. K. Kushwaha, Raja Ram Pal and L. C. Kol (Congress), and Manoj Kumar (RJD). One was a Rajya Sabha member – the BJP's C. S. Lodha.

10. The other case heard related to Rajya Sabha member Sakal Maharaj of Samajwadi Party who was expelled for his involvement in the MP Local Area Development (MPLAD) fund scam.

The above story relates to a sting operation in which a few members of Parliament were caught accepting money for asking questions in the Parliament. The Lok Sabha and Rajya Sabha had expelled these members after committees appointed by two Houses found them guilty and suggested expulsion. The members filed a petition in the Supreme Court. The Court issued notices to the two pressing officers seeking information. Both the presiding officers refused to accept the notice. A confrontation was expected but the Supreme Court averted it by upholding the right of the House to expel members if found guilty.

The first three paragraphs of the story explain the main judgment of the Supreme Court. It also gives the background and the main focus that a conflict between the judiciary and legislature has been averted. However, the fourth and fifth paragraphs are the twist in the story. Though the Court upheld the right of legislative bodies to expel their members, it refused to accept that the Parliament's actions were not subject to judicial review. This is crucial to the story. The person who misses it will not be able to understand that though the Court has given the right to Parliament to expel their members it has retained the right to review parliamentary decisions. Paragraphs six to ten give other details of the judgment to provide base to the story. These five paragraphs develop the story in the pyramid form.

This style is called 'hourglass' because an inverted pyramid is placed on the top of a pyramid with a link that can be in the shape of a narrow rectangle or square. It is named so because the figure resembles an hourglass that was used to measure time in the old days.

Focus Style

The focus style was designed and developed mainly for the front-page stories by American newspapers. This style follows the story telling approach in developing a news story. In a way it is similar to the hourglass style. Nevertheless, it is different in more than one way. The hourglass style requires that the main news be told in the beginning. But this is not the case in the focus style. In this technique the main news should not be revealed in the first few paragraphs. These paragraphs should only focus on some person, event or situation. The story should be allowed to expand in these paragraphs. Unlike the inverted pyramid style where the lead is confined to one paragraph, the lead in the focus style is allotted more space. In an important story it may even take four to five paragraphs. The lead should include details of the person, place, situation or event. It may include information that may not be newsworthy at all.

After the lead the story would present the focus or the central point of the story in two to three paragraphs. The central point should be described in detail. It should take two to three paragraphs. This part of the focus story is known as the nutgraph and is synergised with the lead. In fact, the lead should explain by example the central point in the core paragraph. The main issue around which the story is woven is developed in these paragraphs. In fact, this portion of the whole write up makes the story newsworthy.

The last part of the story is the conclusion. In the American manner of speech it is called the 'kicker.' It contains two to three paragraphs, which are used to wind up the story. The kicker or conclusion should be related to the person, place, situation or event that was described in the lead.

The focus style has an advantage of flexibility. A perceptive and sensitive editor can evolve and unfold the same story in a number of ways. As the story begins with the specifics and then goes into generality, an astute reporter and an imaginative editor can develop a lively and thought-provoking story. The focus style is suitable for political, business and cultural stories. Sports writers use it frequently with creativity. The success of the story, however, depends on the selection of the lead and the development of lead paragraphs. Sometimes the story begins well with an interesting and relevant lead but loses focus when the core paragraph is written. The mismatch between the lead and the core paragraph must be meticulously and fastidiously avoided as it may completely bewilder the reader.

Example:
We give here an example of how a sensitive and provoking interest of general concern should be edited using the focus style. This is the story reporting the court judgement in the first of the 19 cases of rape and murder including 15 children and three women of the Nithari killings that came to limelight towards the end of 2006 when skeletons were dug out from a drain outside D-5 of Sector 31, the house of Mohinder Pandher.

Example:
1. Fifty-five-year-old earthmoving equipment dealer, Mohinder Pandher and his 33-year-old domestic help Surendra Koli reacted in contrasting ways on Friday as a CBI judge pronounced capital punishment to both of them.

2. Koli, who had confessed to slashing the body of 14-year-old Rimpa Halder before eating cooked portions from the victim's breast and an arm, seemed keen on appealing against the verdict. Within minutes of the sentencing, he was seen asking for a copy of the judgement. "I want to read the judgement?" he told the court staff.

3. Pander, who was given a clean chit by the CBI as he was in Australia when the murder was allegedly committed, told his wife that he doesn't want to appeal in a higher court. "Please don't appeal," Pandher told Devander Kaur his wife for 30 years, as she held his hand. "Let it be over, please, no appeals now," a composed-looking Pandher added, as police constables moved the two convicts out of the packed courtroom.

4. The verdict is the first of the 19 cases of rape and murder including 15 children and three women of the Nithari sensational killings case that shocked the country over two years ago. In December 2006 there was nationwide revulsion after police recovered skulls, bones and body parts of 19 children and young women, who had allegedly been sexually exploited, from a drain behind Pandher's D-5 house in Noida's Sector 31.

Editing the Main Story

5. Karandeep Singh, Pandher's 25-year-old son had told a newspaper before the sentence that he would prefer a capital punishment. "I'd rather that my father is awarded a capital punishment. There are 18 other cases which will be fought on the same evidence and my father will be doomed in jail for his entire life," Karandeep had said. But Karandeep's mother, after the verdict was delivered, reacted differently and said she would not give up and would fight till the end to prove Pandher innocent

6. "Which man does not have a one-night stand these days? Who does not sleep with call girls?" I accept these allegations may be true. But my husband cannot kill anyone nor can he ever sexually exploit a child," said an emotionally charged Kaur.

7. "There is something for which only my mother can hold him guilty. Not the media, not a court of law," said Karandeep, who left a course in political science at the University of Windsor in Canada to fight his father's case.

8. Karandeep held media responsible for the harsh judgement and said his father was a victim of media trial. "It has been proved beyond doubt that my dad was in Australia at the time of the incident. The CBI itself has ruled out his involvement but because of media pressure, my father was dragged into the case again," he said.

9. Pandher was under relentless stress during his custody and developed diabetes. He is now being given insulin twice a day. The family alleged that the case had been made out as a "rich versus poor" issue. "If a servant is indulging in a crime in your absence why are you holding the employer responsible?" Kaur said. "We never suspected his intentions and activities. I lived in that house (D-5, Sector 31) from 2000 to 2005, but I could never suspect what all Koli has been doing. The house was always spic and span. Koli is clever man and he knows what to say and what not to," Kaur added.

10. The family also narrated the trauma they underwent looking for a lawyer to defend Pandher. "Criminal lawyers

would hang up on us the moment we mentioned Nithari. A few demanded fees as high as Rs. 50 lakh to consider his case," Kaur said.

It is clear that the story does not start with the lead. It focuses on two persons, Pandher and Koli the two convicts given death sentence. The following two paragraphs (02 and 03) provide the lead. It talks about the crime and the reaction of the two on the court judgement. The next five paragraphs (04 to 08) describe the central point or the focus of the story. They describe the case, the judgement, and the reaction of the wife and son of Pandher. The last two paragraphs (09 and 10) are the conclusion showing how sad the family of Pandher was.

Narrative Style

The narrative style of writing is a blend of the journalistic and literary styles. It is called creative non-fiction writing also, as it is similar to literary writing. It is most appropriate for soft stories that do not contain much hard news because narrative touches such as dialogues and absorbing descriptions can make even a dull news story interesting. These stories are not typical news stories and, therefore, should not be written in the inverted pyramid or hourglass style. Conversely, a narrative writing style is the most suitable for developing these stories. Stories edited using this style become popular because of the liberal use of intimate accounts of people as they live their daily lives. Such stories describe universal human characteristics and experiences in a pleasant way. These may range from incredible to pleasant-sounding and from relaxing to nerve-racking.

The narrative story has two components: A story; and narration of the story or storytelling. This technique of writing a story or a novel is used in storytelling. The news for this type of story should be collected from different people. They should be approached and interviewed to get materials for the story. Wide-ranging and comprehensive research is essential for such stories, to collect detailed information so that the depictions are as accurate as reality. They must tell how the events developed and what their experiences were. It would give a realistic touch to the story and seem as if the readers themselves were witnessing the events like riots, battles and police action. Nevertheless, the success of a narrative story depends on the depth of reporting. A journalist who has not attentively gathered details and quotations will find it difficult to narrate the story in this style. The desk-editor when using this technique of editing should know how narrative stories are to be written. He should refer the story back to the reporter if he finds missing gaps or the need of some on-the-spot information. An imaginative and creative editor can convert even a dull story into a very readable and interesting one.

The narrative style has been in use in newspapers for a long time. This technique is most suitable for writing three types of stories.

First, the ones in which the narrative can be strong. These are stories in which the events are recreated as they happened. One good example is the story of how Vijay, a business tycoon, contemplates different ways to keep rivals on the back foot.

The story:

> An ancient king of Greece, Dionysius, about two thousand years ago, found a unique way to teach a lesson to a critical and go-getting courtier. The king invited him to become the king for a day. When the courtier occupied the throne he found a sword hanging over his head. Every time the unfortunate courtier, Damocles, looked up, he saw the grim symbol of a monarch's fluctuating fortunes.
>
> Vijay, the ostentatious 'king of good times', is also contemplating different ways to keep his rivals on the run. Though he does not have to worry about ambitions staff, like Dionysius, eying at his job, there are rivals inviting Vijay's wrath. Vijay decided to swing into action when a global beer giant Hans took control of Scottish & Newcastle (S & N), threatening to make an entry into Vijay's Company (VC); S & N has a substantial share in VC.
>
> Vijay discussed and evaluated various options with his legal team before launching his assault. S & N had several special privileges and rights on VC's board. Vijay wanted

that Hans should not inherit the benefits that were being enjoyed by S & N. He had no problems about Hans as a partner but wanted it to work out a separate agreement on rights and privileges with him.

Therefore to preempt Hans, Vijay and his group of companies filed a suit in the Bombay High Court against Hans and certain employees of S & N, seeking termination of the special privileges granted to S & N under the deal. They also wanted a permanent order and injunction, restraining S & N employees from seeking any confidential information about VC, and from carrying out duties as directors of VC.

At first glance, it would appear that VC is itching for an intense fight with Hans. It would also appear that Vijay, with his larger-than-life image and fondness for taking the battle to the opposition camp, is sounding the bugle for a long-drawn-out encounter with Hans. But when deeply analysed it does not appear to be so. Vijay's move seems to be a carefully planned tactic to protect his flanks, exploit the legal options available and put pressure on Hans to come to an agreement with him.

This is a good example of how stories that have fast movement and conflict of interest should be told. It recounts how a far-sighted business tycoon handles his rival so that his business interests do not suffer. If told in a routine way it would not have much impact.

Secondly, the narrative style should be used to edit those stories where the reporter should perform the role of a narrator. Such stories are not easy to edit because the reporter may not just remain a narrator. He may be tempted to make *himself* the centre of the story. Here is an example of editing a story in which the reporter acts as a narrator and tells how the police officer who impressed by Dhoni made him pay a fine for violating traffic rules:

The story:

For Saifuddin Ahmed, posted at a busy Ranchi roundabout, it was business as usual on Tuesday when he flagged down a black SUV that had dark tinted windows, which are not allowed under the Bihar traffic rules. But when the car stopped and the driver rolled down the window glass, the traffic policeman's jaw dropped.

"*Aree aap hai* (Oh, it's you), was all the sheepish traffic constable could muster on seeing cricket sensation and Jharkhand's hero, Mahendra Singh Dhoni behind the wheel of the Scorpio.

Brushing back his locks, Dhoni, who was wearing dark glasses, accepted the awe-struck cop's admiration. It was usual for him to face such situations. But the confident cop, though over-awed wanted Dhoni to explain the violation of rule.

Dhoni pleaded that he needed to be shielded from public glare because of his popularity and requested to be let off. That's true, because had Dhoni stepped out of his SUV onto to the Ranchi thoroughfare, he would have been mobbed the way he was when he had strolled into a local beauty salon for a haircut in November. Police had to intervene to disperse his fans.

But on Tuesday morning, Ahmed having regained his self-control pointed out that the Ranchi Administration had banned dark films on windows and windscreens in December. When Dhoni tried again to explain that he used tinted glasses due to security concerns, Ahmed reached out to shake hands with the wicket keeper, but firmly said, "Sir, you will have to pay the mandatory fine of Rs 900".

Realising the cop wouldn't budge, Dhoni paid up and chose to slip out before he attracted a large crowd at the busy intersection.

This story has been narrated as if the reporter were present on the scene. The details are graphic and dialogues give the whole story a realistic touch.

The third use of the narrative technique is the stylistic experiment. Here the structure, chronology or syntax is used in such a way that the reading becomes interesting and enjoyable. A good example of editing a story in this style was the one when Barack Obama won the democratic nomination in May 2008 for the forthcoming US presidential election in November.

The story:

From a dark horse in the Democrat race to the first black US presidential candidate from a major party, Mr. Barack Obama has had a meteoric rise from political obscurity to be at a sniffing distance of the White House.

The 46-year-old Harvard-educated first-time Senator from Illinois had a prolonged bitter battle with powerful Democrat rival Hillary Clinton for winning the nomination—a roller-coaster run that was dominated by frequent controversies mostly related to his race and religion.

Son of a father who travelled from a small Kenyan village to pursue University education in Hawaii and went on to marry a white woman from Kansas, Obama started his political career as a low-paid community organiser. The Columbia University graduate and the first African-American president of the Harvard Law Review served for eight years in the Illinois state Senate.

In 2004, he entered the Capitol Hill after a landslide Senate election victory and soon became a media darling and one of the most visible figures in Washington, with two best-selling books to his name.

The father of two young daughters, who appeared with his wife Michelle to declare victory before a cheering crowd in St Paul today, described it as a "defining moment" for the nation which abolished slavery 200 years ago but is still battling the scourge of racial discrimination. "Tonight we mark the end of the one historic journey with the beginning of another—a journey that will bring a new and better day to America", Obama, who projected himself as a candidate for "change," said.

"America, this is our moment. This is our time. Our time to turn the page on policies of the past," he pledged.

The Hawaii-born Obama's father, the Barack Obama Sr., as also the Indonesian Man his mother married after divorcing, were Muslim. During the vicious campaign,

Obama had to reiterate that he is a devout Christian and attended secular and Catholic schools rather than a madrassa for the four years he lived in Indonesia, a largely Muslim country.

"The journey will be difficult… if we are willing to work for it… then I am absolutely certain that generations from now, we will be able to look back and tell our children that this was the moment when we began to provide care for the sick and good jobs to the jobless…this was the moment when we ended a war and secured our nation and restored our image," Obama said in his victory speech.

It is a good example where the desk-editor has converted the reporter's copy into an interesting and enjoyable story. It uses structure, syntax and chronology in such a way that the story becomes highly readable.

Editing a narrative style story is not easy. It is the most difficult assignment as it requires a good experience of creative writing. Moreover, he edits a story that was not witnessed by him. In the above story, though the desk-editor was thousands of kilometres away from the place of the incident, he has been able to create the excitement of victory. Only an experienced editor will have the capacity and capability to revise, correct and rewrite such a story.

It is essential that the desk-editor, when editing a narrative style story, should check the chronology very carefully. He should ensure that the flashbacks are in proper order and the dialogues are at their proper place and do not contradict each other. In such stories it must also be ensured that the beginning is interesting, middle portions are narrative, and the end is dramatic. The three must be in equal proportion. The narrative stories should not be shortened, as trimming such stories would make them monotonous, unexciting and uninteresting.

The narrative technique is usually used in monthly magazines. Hard news, scoops and breaking news cannot be written in the narrative style. Nevertheless, it can be a good change from the dull inverted pyramid style, particularly for weekends and Sunday editions.

General Precautions when Editing the Body of a News Story

A desk-editor uses different techniques for editing different stories for the same-day edition. Each requires a different skill set. Ever desk-editor learns it whether by trial and error or with the help of the peer group. Nevertheless, there are certain precautions that every desk-editor must observe while editing different stories, irrespective of the technique used for editing that particular story. Here are a few general precautions that must be followed when editing the body of a news story.

Transitions

Moving from one fact to another in a story is known as transition. It should be effortless and natural. The progression of a thought should be normal and the sequence of facts and action rational, reasonable and acceptable. Changeover or transition in stories helps the reader to move from one fact to the next in an easily understandable way that should not only be smooth but also be in a logical order. Reporters seldom care for easy transition. The desk-editors have to pay attention to this aspect of writing.

> Example: The Union Minister for External Affairs, Pranab Mukherjee criticised the hanging of Saddam. Mukherjee said that the trial should have been fair.

The reporter repeats the name of the Union Minister for External Affairs. It should be edited to: The Union Minster for External Affairs, Pranab Mukherjee criticised the hanging of Saddam, as the trial was not fair.

Identifying news

News should be properly identified in the first or the second paragraph. Many desk-editors are not careful. They edit the story in such a way that readers are unable to find out the main news, information or facts even in the first few paragraphs.

An example can be given. The following story as reported by a daily tabloid is an example of ambiguous editing. The story is

Editing the Main Story

on the new BJP government in Karnataka (late May 2008) that won the trust vote when the first session began in early June. The reader after reading the whole story does not know how the voting was conducted and by how many votes the Government won the confidence vote.

The story:

> A week after assuming office, B. S. Yeddyurappa, the BJP's first southern chief minister, finally heaved a sign of relief on Friday. His government won the vote of confidence in the Karnataka assembly with ease.
>
> Unlike last time when the BJP depended heavily on its coalition partner, the JU(S), for support during the trust vote, Yeddyurappa exuded confidence this time. He let go of the green shawl that he had been clutching since the day of the swearing-in.
>
> The opposition parties, Congress and the JD(S), which together have 108 members against the BJP's 110, chose not to give the ruling party a hard time. But the Congress staged a walkout.
>
> Opposition leader Mallikarjun M. Khage and senior Congress MLA Siddaramaiah took the occasional dig at the BJP's wafer thin-majority – courtesy the support of six independent legislators. "If three of your MLAs are missing anytime during the legislature session, can you imagine your plight?" Siddaramaiah said.

Another national broadsheet daily took care of these lapses and reported that the voting was by voice, vote that requires no counting. The story as reported:

The story:

> The week-old BJP Government in Karnataka, lead by Chief Minister B S Yeddyurappa, on Friday cleared its first hurdle by sailing through confidence motion with the support of six Independent MLAs in the legislative Assembly.
>
> The confidence motion was moved by Chief Minister Yeddyurappa a few hours after Governor Rameshwar

> Thakur addressed a joint session of the state legislature and outlined the policy agenda of the new Government.
>
> The confidence motion put through a voice vote, was a foregone conclusion given the BJP's numerical strength of 110 MLAs and the firm support of six Independents—that eased the party, pass the simple mark of 113.

The broadsheet story is better edited as it gives all the necessary details connected with the news. It tells that the voting was through voice vote after the address by the Governor.

Explain Unfamiliar Words

Many newspaper stories contain words and terms that are not known or understood by ordinary readers. The desk-editor should change such words. If that is not possible, as it may affect the substance of the story, these should be explained in a manner that readers are able to understand them. Various methods can be used to do this. First is to explain the meaning of the term or phrase in brackets. Second the phrase can be explained in simple language immediately after its use. It can be set off with a coma, colon or dash. The third way is to write the explanation in the next sentence. Most technical stories are made understandable by using this technique.

An example:

> The declaration of emergency came after the UN had suspended all technical support for elections that have been boycotted by the opposition and are looking increasingly chaotic and possibly untenable.
>
> Technical support includes consulting and advice on publishing results as well as ballot casting and counting.

Give Examples

Desk editors can make a story more interesting and readable by giving real life examples. Examples are all the more needed in abstract stories. A story on juvenile crime may give the reasons for such crime, percentage of juveniles' committing crime, a breakup of crimes committed by them, and the gender ratio. The story would be dull and drab if only these facts and data are mentioned. It, however, would become more interesting if the cases of one or two juveniles involved in crimes are mentioned.

Add Humour

Readers always look for humour in a story, even in the fearful ones. If some humour were added at an appropriate place to a story, it would become more attractive. But do not overdo it. A mere hint may be more effective than elaborating it.

Points to Remember

The most important information should be mentioned in the lead.

While editing the story include all details that you think will interest and affect readers of your newspaper.

Try to develop, by using the power of your language and expression, imagery of the whole situation and happenings.

The second paragraph should expand the lead further.

Avoid leapfrogging by giving a one- or two-word transition from the lead to the name in the second paragraph.

Your sentences should be confusion-free, precise and to the point.

Do not use the same structure of sentence again and again. Keep changing it.

Do not use too many words to explain the same thing.

Mention all the major issues in the first paragraph so that the reader can understand the whole situation.

Movement from one paragraph to another should be smooth and logical.

Use something interesting to sustain the interest of the readers in the story.

Try to be specific. Try not to involve generalities that have to be explained later.

When you have finished editing, read the story again and critically edit it if it lacks sharpness.

References:

A History of News, Mitchell Stephens, Quoted by Cheryl Gibbs & Tom Warhover in Getting the Whole Story: Reporting & Writing the News (The Guitford Press).

Reporting for the Media, Fred Fedler, John R. Bender, Lucinda D. Davenport and Michael W. Drager (Oxford University Press, New York and Oxford).

6
Heading or Headline Writing

When the train stopped at a railway station in the afternoon, a hawker came running shouting the headline: 'The maid ran away with the police constable.' Passengers in the railway compartment were inquisitive to read the news. Therefore, every one purchased a copy of the tabloid. As the passengers were searching for the news the train started moving.

There was neither news nor headline.

The purpose of the above story, which is popular in the newsrooms, is to give you an idea about how headings or headlines help in obtaining a larger sale of an evening tabloid.

The most important selling point is the headline to a news story in a newspaper.. Every desk-editor should use all his expertise in providing a good headline to a story. He should try and be straightforward because a headline narrates the substance of the story to the reader. If a sub-heading is given along with the main heading, it should have some relation to the story and its heading. But the same phrasing should not be used in both the headings. If that is done it would not only be bad editing but also a sheer waste of space.

The Headline

The headline is the soul of a story as it could make or break it. A newspaper page is always crowded with competitive stories and the role of the headline is to attract the attention of the reader to select the story for reading. An interesting and provocative headline will seek the attention of the reader. Silently it would be saying: "Read me, how can you ignore me?" In other words, headlines help a reader to scan the newspaper quickly and effectively and decide which story to read and which not to.

Writing headlines and allied items like cross headings, side heads, straplines, are the creative branches of desk-editing. These are known as the 'page furniture' in American journalism and are meant to project the news story or the article.

Headlines draw the maximum attention of the reader and therefore are the most important of all the other items. A desk-editor, hence, has to give his best in creating imaginative headings to a story. Some desk-editors give a longer time to headline writing and come up with creative headlines. But this again depends on the quality of the copy received from the reporter. The lucky desk-editors get clean and good copies and so have to spend less time in working on them in improving them further. The time saved is then fruitfully spent in headline writing. Many may not be so lucky and so spend most of their time in editing the story. They are left with less time to decide about the headline. Nevertheless, they have to do their best in projecting the story.

After checking the copy for accuracy, clarity, conciseness, unanswered questions, consistency of style and tone, the desk-editor's next job is to write the headline.

> Headlines are 'display windows' of the newspaper.
> Nevertheless, their function is more than that.

The headline, in fact, is the principal source of information The majority of newspaper readers cannot spare much time in the morning for reading the newspaper. The average time spent on reading a newspaper is not more than half an hour. Many would finish the paper in just five minutes, particularly those who read more than one newspaper. Senior political leaders, bureaucrats, corporate heads, professors, journalists and the like fall in this category. Such people do not have the time or need to read each and every news item in detail. They just scan through the newspaper, concentrating on headlines, and speed-read the news that they feel might be useful and interesting. The headline helps them decide which news item might be useful to them. By reading the headline they come to know the nature and intensity of the news and then accordingly select items, articles and features for speed-reading.

The headline has two functions to perform. Firstly, it has to attract the attention of the reader and invite him to scan the story. Secondly, it forms an element in the typographical pattern of the page.

The first function, drawing the attention of the reader, is more important than the first one; still the second governs the first one. It governs the first function by determining the type size and width, limiting by the choice of words that a desk-editor can use. That is the reason that many times the night-editor or the chief sub-editor changes the best headlines that were creatively thought up by the desk-editor. Still there are instances when the night-editor has changed the type on the page to accommodate the original headline. However, this happens seldom. The visualising that goes into a page, particularly of page-one, is a well-thought out exercise. It is considered to be important in itself and is designed to suit the stories it contains. Therefore, not many editors allow this to be changed for the sake of one headline.

In the main stories, the headlines are normally decided in advance and written as part of the page strategy. However, the freedom to desk-editors to use the type and space in the remaining pages provides a challenge to their headline-writing skills.

Headlines have a few more functions. Firstly, different headlines compete with each other in attracting the attention of a reader. Since the reader has limited time to read the newspaper, the headline helps him in determining whether or not to go beyond it. Majority of the readers may overlook even the best story if the headline is lousy, not understandable or uninteresting.

Secondly, a headline in its various forms is essential to make the pages eye-catching, balanced and attractive. Therefore, the headline provides ingredients of an attractive display package.

Thirdly, the headline provides character and stability to the newspaper. The consistent use of familiar headline families and styles, gives the newspaper a relatively friendly and welcome personality.

Lastly, it helps at the newsstands in selling the newspaper. Catchy headlines shouted by vendors on streets attract passersby to buy the newspapers. Tabloids and evening newspapers depend on headlines as the main selling technique.

The Rules

A few points should be kept in mind while writing a headline. Good headlines should be written in a condensed and telegraphic language as these are meant to attract the attention of the reader immediately. Also the headlines have to be fitted in the allotted space. A good headline-writer's skill lies in finding short, direct and concrete words and not long, indirect and abstract ones for creative headlines in the minimum possible time. However, short, direct and concrete words should be used carefully and not mindlessly. The words, in fact, should be such that the desk editor is able to convey exactly what the story intends to convey.

Three Components of a Headline:

Compact; short and snappy; and fits in the allotted space.

A good headline should:
Attract the readers' attention.
Summarise the story.
Depict the mood of the story.
Help set the tone of the newspaper.
Provide adequate typographic relief.

The headline must be drawn from information in the first paragraph of the story. The key words should be selected to fit in the allotted space. Normally, if it is possible, a noun should be followed by a verb and both placed in the top line. A non-verb headline can be used if it sets the appropriate tone for the story. In fact, it is more suitable for features. Adjectives and adverbs are also not used in headings. These can be used in feature headlines. An active verb should invariably be preferred.

The desk-editor should try to capture the vivacity of the story and reflect it in the headline. The headline should be written in a minimum number of words and the language should be simple. Words used in the headline should be short, direct and concrete and not long, indirect or abstract. Various alternate words to explain a situation should always be kept in mind and used judiciously. If the main focus point is *'abandon'* you have to keep in mind the various words like:

> **Drop; give up; quit; skip; yield; desert; leave; neglect; pull out; etc.**

Clichés

Stereotyped words or phrases are known as clichés. These ideas or expressions have been used again and again so much in the past that they have become outdated. Many are 300 years old and have lost their relevance in the new cultural, social and political environment. Even those words or phrases that are new have been used so much during the past 30 years that they neither entertain nor amaze anyone. Therefore they are meaningless and do not create an impact. One such cliché is the 'TINA factor'. It was used in the seventies to indicate a situation in which "there is no alternative to the ruling Congress government at the Centre"; it was not popular and people wanted to get rid of it. Another such cliché is YUPPI—young Punjabi urbanite.

Desk-editors should also avoid stale jargon words, like 'see you later'. Some short words have become clichés and are often used by desk-editors. A few examples: 'axe' for 'cancel' or 'sack';

'quit' for 'leave' or 'resign'; 'vow' for 'promise'; 'slam' for 'criticise'; 'shun' for 'avoid'. These should be avoided if the copy is to be different and discreet.

Here is short list of clichés that should be avoided:

comfort level	wake-up call	sea change
spirited chase	angry mob	blind as a bat
cool as a cucumber	landed the job	
lying in the pool	a step in the right	a close brush with
test the waters	whirlwind campaign	spin doctors
round the clock	bare minimum	blessing in disguise
caught red-handed	calm before the storm	came under fire
complete stranger	crystal clear	
curate's egg	dime a dozen	doomed to fail
dream come true	drop in the ocean	dying specie
fell on deaf ears	foreseeable future	grief-stricken
Hobson's choice	last but not least	line of fire
lodge a complaint	miraculous escape	necessary evil
opened fire	pillar of strength	paved the way
pitched battle	police dragnet	proud parents
reign of terror	share a joke	smell a rat
spread like wildfire	sudden death	still at large
took its toll	time will tell	tip of the iceberg
tracked down	under siege	word of caution

Headlines should be in current colloquial English that is be easily understood by the readers without much trouble. Never use tabloid jargon in broadsheet.

Some phrases, such as: 'The British are coming' (any British success in another country) or YUPPI (any successful person who is a young Punjabi professional) are endlessly used and reused and show no novelty. Examples are:

The Chinese are coming!

(Flooding of the Indian market by the Chinese goods.)

YUPPIs invade USA

(The success of a large number of young Punjabi professionals in the United States.)

Other Precautions

Headline words that have been used too much, like "Businessman shot dead" should be avoided in giving headlines to your stories. Regular readers of the newspaper may be reading it again and again and may get annoyed and become apathetic to these headlines.

As headlines should be crisp and short, abbreviations are rarely used in writing headlines and cross heads. For example a heading, "Re hits 2-mts low" looks messy, apart from being incomprehensible to many readers.

Punctuation should also be kept out of headlines and cross heads. Commas, dashes, exclamation marks and quotes look untidy. If at all these are to be used, their utilisation should be less than that in the text. Some papers use white space to indicate punctuation. But now this is outdated.

There are no well-set rules for using capital (caps) and lower case letters. Some newspapers use only capitals in headings, particularly on the first page. All-cap headlines are used for very important stories. For example after the Satyam Computers scam, the Government dismissed its Board and appointed a new one with three members. One newspaper carried the following headline for the lead story:

SATYAM BOARD DISMISSED
A NEW ONE APPOINTED

Most of the newspapers through out the world usually follow the practice of using uppers and lowers. But in very important news a newspaper may use the headline in two lines, using caps in first line and lower in the second. For example when Barack Obama assumed presidency in November 2008 one newspaper gave the following heading:

CHANGE IN
White House

Capital letters can be used after a colon in headlines and cross heads. For example:

Budget: Delhi gets Rs. 2,148 crore

The headline invariably has to be phrased in the present tense. It should say what has happened or is happening.

For example:

Pakistan gives in to Taliban

It cannot be "Pakistan gave in to Taliban". The use of past tense dates the story in which majority of the readers become disinterested, particularly in headlines for hard news.

Personal names should be avoided unless the person is very prominent and is well known nationally, like the Prime Minister or the President. Names can also be used if they are vital news elements in themselves. For example:

Suit against Renuka over 'Taliban' jibe

This heading was given to a story that indicated that the Mayor of Mangalore filed a criminal case against the Union Women and Child Development Minister, Renuka Chowdhury for her comment that the city has been "Talibanised".

Local newspapers liberally use personal names in their headlines. The reason is the circulation is confined to the city or town and most of the people know the person being mentioned.

Some newspapers have laid down rules that in a heading the lines should not end in 'a', 'the', or with 'in'. There is no justification to such a rule as many good headlines may be impaired in an attempt to conform to this rule. A better, reasonable and logical rule may be that a heading that requires a secondary line (also know as a 'tag-line') to explain or justify it, should not be used. In such a case the heading should be written in such a way that the tag-line is merged in the headline.

Sometimes a certain part of or the whole headline is in quotes. It is done when the words have been used by someone else and they may be politically powerful and the newspaper does not want to associate itself or agree with the opinion expressed. For example:

Sonia's gloves off: 'Gujarat run by liars, peddlers of religion & death'

Heading or Headline Writing 115

The quotation marks in the heading (only single and not double quotation marks are used in headlines) makes it clear that someone other than the newspaper is making the assertion. The above heading was given by a newspaper in December 2007 to report the speech that Mrs. Sonia Gandhi delivered at Chilhli and Jasdan in Gujarat before the Assembly elections. In the speech she had said that the Gujarat Government was being run by those who are 'liars, corrupt and peddlers of religion and death'. This practice is followed when reporting political speeches and court matters. The quote marks make it clear that the headline refers to the claim of one party in the courtroom.

Mafia involved in 'Murder'

The headline should always select the precise words to convey the exact meaning. The effort should be to condense the entire story in one or two words. That is, each word should be specific, as there is no place for vagueness in a heading. A word that conveys the exact meaning and condenses the entire story in one or two words should always be preferred than words that may be unclear, confused or inappropriate.

Lastly, the headline must neither be too short nor too long. It must fit in the allotted space.

Alliterations

The repetition of an initial sound is known as alliteration. It is used in headlines for soft (light) stories. Words used in such headings create a jingle effect. These are not liked by serious readers of the newspaper because they create a trivial and frivolous effect. Examples are:

Speedboat kills
Singer as she
Swims with sons

Though serious readers may not like such headings, young readers who like fun and frolic prefer to read such headings in the newspaper. Therefore, the use of alliterations should not be completely barred. However, precautions should be taken that there is no ridiculous use of initials. For example:

> Angry Indians,
> Out of the match,
> Assail Umpire
> At Kolkata

The heading, even when alliterations are used, should be explicit. It should be definite and should clearly and fully explain the main element of the news. There should be no doubt left in the mind of the reader about what happened. An example:

> **Tragic Loss in Fire**

Strapline

Strap means a strip to fasten things together or keep something in place. In journalism a strapline is used to tighten the headline. It is used to support the headline and give it further strength. The need for a strapline is to enable the reader, who is looking at a page or double spread, to know exactly what is happening. A strapline is the second headline that is meant to further explain the story.

Two headlines to a story are given when the story is very important. In such a situation one line is the main headline and the second line is the sub-heading. A sub-heading can be over the main headline or below it. The sub-heading that is given above the main heading is known as 'over-line' or 'upper-deck'. It is known as 'stand-first' in the American and British journalistic terminology. The sub-heading below the main headline is known as 'second deck' or 'subhead'.

You give a second headline when you do not want to incorporate basic information in the main heading. In such a situation you can use the strap line or sub-heading to be more allusive and clever. For instance, if you have interviewed someone who is a well-known person then your heading can say 'Interview with Rahul Gandhi.'

Your stand-first or upper deck then can say what Rahul Gandhi is all about, as well as introduce the interviewer: 'Utter Pradesh is going back economically' etc. It can also tell readers more about what Rahul Gandhi is like: 'The P.M. in waiting' or 'The dynastic rule continues'. The objective is to use the various elements to ensure that between them they provide all the necessary information.

The main headline is selected first and contains the most important, immediate, dramatic point. An example:

> Computer giant hit by global slowdown
> Indian jobs at Risk as Wipro
> Lays off 10,000

The secondary headline provides context, explains and gives the background.

> Karsevaks Storm Babri Masjid
> Violence erupts all over India.

Two headlines are an essential element of the feature or the story package. These are good and useful for readers because they can easily identify precisely what the feature or story is all about in the first 50 words. These headlines also indicate the tone of what is to follow. Brevity is of the essence. Most contemporary strap lines should not be more than a single punchy sentence, two if the writer's by-line is to be incorporated.

Unique Stories

Many a times the desk-editor is given a unique story to edit. Giving an unusual headline is a creative task in such a situation. In November 2005 the following news story appeared in a newspaper:

> A sheikh taxi driver in a Saudi Arabia village married four girls in one ceremony. All the four were teachers in a local school. The driver used to take them to school, as females were not allowed to drive in Saudi Arabia.
>
> The four decided to marry the same man as they were overwhelmed by his conduct and behaviour and they did not want to give up the benefit of being driven to the school.

The desk-editor gave the following headline that was appreciated very much by the professionals and the readers:

Meet the wife
Four of them

Skills necessary for creative headlines

The perception of the story should be fully understood.
The vocabulary should be accurate.
The heading must convey exactly the true purpose of the story.
The sentence structure should be sharp, precise and clear.
The use of words that may offend the readers' sensitivity should be avoided.

Writing A Headline

Writing a headline is an art and there is no fixed formula to suggest how it should be written. A well-written story suggests its own headline when it is being edited. However, in many stories it requires much thinking and playing with key words until something comes up as a creative and appealing headline. Many a times the desk-editor is not able to think of a good headline. In such a situation he should consult a senior desk-editor. In every newspaper there are desk-editors who specialise in innovative headings. Their assistance should be taken.

Though there is no fixed formula to guide how to write a headline, two approaches can be used to write headings. The first one is the *factual approach*. The headline indicates the important factual point in the story. It indicates the exact news in the story. For example, there is a plane crash in which all passengers die. The headline, using the factual approach, can be written as following:

All Die in
Plane Crash

The second is known as the *oblique approach*. This approach is used mainly in writing headings to soft stories, particularly fun stories about film stars, popular singers or even pets. Such headlines immediately suggest an interesting story. For example there was a story of a person who found the milk pouch missing in the morning when he opened the door to collect it. It happened for a few days. He finally decided to catch the thief. He got up early in the morning and kept a watch through the magic eye on the door. He saw the milkman leaving the milk pouch at the door. A few minutes later he saw a dog picking up the pouch and running away with it. He told the story to a journalist friend of his who thought it was a good light story for the Sunday edition of his paper. The desk-editor gave the following heading:

The Milk-thief is caught
It's the dog

Desk-editors generally prefer the factual approach in writing headlines. The oblique approach should be used sparingly. If it is used widely, as in tabloids, the newspaper looks frivolous. It is indeed irritating for a serious reader to face too many headlines of an oblique nature. It may put him off from reading the newspaper. Therefore, a balance must be maintained even in tabloids.

Headline Typography

A headline should fulfill two conditions: it should be easy to read and attract the readers' attention; and, it must look typographically attractive. A desk-editor has very little choice in selecting the size and width of the type because it is chosen to fulfil a design element. In other word it has to match the other types and contribute to the character of the page. Nevertheless, he has complete freedom in composing the headline. He should use this freedom to compose the headline in such a way that it has an intrinsic balance of its own. He should be careful to see that each line is of the right width within the permitted measure. The line should have the sufficient number of letters so that it is not too narrow. It should also not be too wide because of too many letters. The lines of the heading should match and not deform the page design.

In the newspaper parlance the story is always linked with the number of words. When the editor decides on the story, he also decides the number of words to be given to it. If you have seen the movie, *Page-3*, it showed the editor asking the reporter to give a story by the evening in 300 words. This is a normal practice in the newspaper realm. This is always done to fit a story in the given space that depends on the importance of the story. The same goes for the headline. A headline should have only that many words so as to fit in the allotted space.

The number of words in a headline is important. In fact, word count in a heading is more important than the word count in the main story. The reason is that the desk-editor has to deal with anything from 6 to about 12 words in headlines of between 18-points and 36-points across a single column. In streamers or banners (prominent headline in large type) or other multi-column headlines, the space for letters is more but the type is larger. Thus, the number of words in a headline across three to six columns may be less than the count for four small lines across a single column. Whatever may be the page situation, desk-editors are required to accommodate the headlines in six to seven words.

The tabloids, now becoming quite popular in India, use bigger and bolder headlines. The desk-editors in these papers find the problem of word count more acute. As the headline has to be fixed in the given space (that is limited because the tabloid is half the size of a broad sheet) without compromising on the punch of the story, the headlines, in many instances, contain distorted phrases and jargons. An example:

MEDIA RAPS GAG BY GOVT

This was a headline when the Information & Broadcasting Minister wanted to introduce the Press Bill in the Lok Sabha to put restrictions on the print and electronic media.

The national newspapers such as *The Times of India, Hindustan Times, The Hindu,* are more sober and conventional in displaying headlines compared to tabloids like *Mail Today,* or *Mid-Day.* They mostly use lower case headlines, except when the news is of vital importance. Excessively wordy headlines are avoided and the extra words available are put to the best use.

The desk-editor should always follow the in-house style sheet and consult the type-book that many newspapers provide to their journalists. Every good newspaper has a type-book that shows the different types (known as 'fonts') and the way they should be used. The types are shown with standard counts, in capital and in lower case, across a single column and also in double, three or even more columns. A newspaper of repute must develop a style sheet and a type book.

Many desk-editors, who may not be familiar with the profession, give an artistic touch to the display by composing the headline in a pyramid shape like the following one:

All

DIE IN

PLANE CRASH

Some may be even more imaginative and give the headline in variable width as below:

THE

MILK THIEF

IS

CAUGHT.

IT'S

THE DOG

The news desk-editor should not let his imagination run riot. He should learn by looking at various headlines and discuss with seniors when in doubt. He should develop a clipping file to keep the different headline samples from different papers for reference. Also, he should consult the type book, if there is any, in the house and use the type in different sizes as prescribed in the book.

Letter Headlines

The 'Letter Page' section in a newspaper is different. It is sober and straightforward and can present a lighter touch at times. The letters addressed to 'The Editor' are opinions, suggestions, appreciations and criticisms. The headline should indicate the tone of the letter and summarise the letter. Quote marks should be avoided since the context makes it clear that the views expressed are not of the paper. For example, for letters on continuing disruption of Parliament can carry the following headline:

Disruption in Parliament Goes on

Breakers

Various devices are used to break the monotony of text on a page so that it looks more interesting and is easier to read. These are—crossheads, side heads, pull quotes and drop caps.

Crossheads are used in the centre of the column and at the beginning of the paragraph. Crossheads are short headings between paragraphs in the body of a feature or story. They should not be more than two or three words long as they are placed only for design purposes and for editorial reasons. Crossheads are placed in the centre of the column.

Side heads are set flush left. The side heads also function as a mini-headline and are used to start a new section. The paragraphs that follow are also set flush left. It can also be after one or two spaces.

Cross heads and side heads should not be used alternately in the newspaper. A format should be laid down and followed meticulously. It should not be changed unless the newspaper is redesigned.

Pull quotes, are also known as 'blurbs'. These should be pulled out from the text and set in a bigger font size. They should be bolder than the body copy and displayed on the page as a teaser for the story. They should not be placed between paragraphs but dropped into the text so that the reader reads across them. The text taken out for the blurb must not be deleted from the text. They are to be set across more than one column and usually given between two rules. They can be edited—shortened and simplified—but the meaning should never be changed.

Drop cap (or sometimes raised) is often used to begin stories and as a visual breaker on the page. These are not used in a daily newspaper. Mostly magazines or Sunday editions use them for feature stories and not for new stories. Certain points have to be kept in mind while using drop caps. One, the sequence of drop caps on a page should be carefully followed and the same letter should not be repeated on the same page. Second, the drop caps should not be combined with a quote. Either the quote mark may be used or the drop cap. When the drop cap is used the sentence may end with a quote mark that shows it a quote. A wise policy would be to rewrite the paragraph and use the quote in the second sentence.

Extras (boxes, tables, graphs, maps, diagrams)

Boxes, panels and sidebars can include simple or complex facts, information, statistics, advice or comments. In general these extras and their visual equivalent—graphs, maps and diagrams—should be planned as an integral part of the story and should not be added at the subbing stage. The purpose of using these extras is to make a story look and read better. It can be done by adding some facts that are missing in the story. In order to make the story more attractive some section can be taken out of the main feature and the material can be given in a box.

Captions

Captions are given to pictures used in the story. A caption should not describe the picture. It should only highlight the main element in the picture. A desk-editor has to be very cautious when writing a caption. He has to ensure that he understands exactly what the cropped picture is depicting. It should be carefully stated in the caption but not in a very direct way. The caption should, where possible, add something to the picture that the visual cannot convey, whether that is actual information—'Minutes before the fatal crash...'—or simply the atmosphere. There is no need to say, 'This picture shows...' You can safely omit the obvious. Readers do expect you to know the identities or the people in a picture. If you do not have their names, or you do not think they are relevant, you need to find a way to explain them in some other way.. Desk-editors should always check that the correct photographs are being used. Two persons in a picture should never be confused. A great care has to be taken if the two are with similar names, particularly if one is a known criminal and the other is an honest person.

Conclusion

Headlines must not create any legal problem for the newspaper. They should be legally safe. Desk-editors should be very careful not to use double-meaning words in their headings. In fact, readers do not like double entendre. They should only be used when they are essential as in satirical or fun stories. Personal names in the headings should be used with great care. One must not play with the name of a person. A play on words based on someone's name is allowed in rare cases but it must be meaningful, humorous and positive. Negative play of words is never allowed.

If the witticism is particularly appealing then it must be integrated with the headline first so that it makes sense. However, never explain a heading that is otherwise meaningless in a strap line. Other types of wit are often more appropriate, including topical or artistic allusion.

Creating headlines to a story or article requires excellent writing skills, a high level of education and awareness, and a sharp verbal intelligence.

A Few Excellent Headlines

Here we give a few examples of ingenious, brilliant and intelligent headlines in newspapers. The following headline was given to the story on the Olympic torch relay run:

DELHI'S CHINESE TORTURE

A newspaper gave the following two-deck heading:

> **Caged torch relay hardly reflects the Olympic spirit**
> **Flame of shame**

Heading or Headline Writing

The story:

At last the long awaited but controversial Olympic torch of the Beijing Olympics Games reached Delhi at mid-night on Thursday April 17 (2008) at 01:10 a.m. from Pakistan. Tight security was provided by a 17-battalion force, along its route from the airport to the Meridian Hotel. The intensive arrangements included a three-layered security around the route of the run. All roads leading to Rashtrapati Bhawan and India Gate were sealed. Not even a bird could enter into the relay track area without proper, prolonged and several security checks.

The Olympic torch was carried through its Delhi leg by tennis stars Leander Paes and Mahesh Bhupati, former hockey players Dhanraj Pillay and Zafar Iqbal, ex-cricketer Bishan Singh Bedi, sprinter P T Usha, weightlifters K Malleswari, and K Kunjurani, hockey star-turned MP Aslam Sher Khan and swimmer Wilson Cherian, besides para-Olympian Rajinder Singh Rahelu. Representing the film fraternity were Saif Ali Khan, Aamir Khan and 'Chak De' girl Sagarika Ghatge.

> The mega event, which was in the last leg here, was reduced to a mere formality as there were virtually no spectators to cheer. Only 200-odd school children and the police personnel witnessed this historic event. The children too were denied entry when their bus was sent back since they were not able to produce identity cards. They were later allowed. The children shouted and cheered the relay with all their might. But soon their cheering meandered to jeering and hooting. And they could not be blamed as they were made to stand in sun and heat for four hours with no water and no shade.

The relay run was completed without any untoward incident. There were no protests and no delays. It was a highly planned and managed affair albeit no spectators and widespread protests by Tibetans all over Delhi. The whole show was like the Republic Day parade, with the tableaux and loud music. It was all neatly conducted but definitely overdone. And the people on the roads paid the price.

As security agencies went on overdrive to secure the Olympic torch relay run, the whole of Delhi underwent a harrowing time. The large number of persons who had to reach their destinations had a traumatic time commuting through the heart of the city as most roads were sealed and cordoned off. The parallel protests and movement in different parts of the city made the situation worse. As the torch made its way back, thousands of airline passengers were stranded in a nightmarish jam on NH-8 well past midnight. Nearly 200 passengers missed their flights and many planes could not take off as the crew was also stranded in the jam.

Another example:
Another good heading to the opening match of the Indian Premier League first 'Twenty-20' match in Bangalore:

>   **The billion-dollar**
>   **Baby is born**
> **Kolkata rock in spectacular IPL opener**

The story was of the Indian Premier League (IPL) cricket that took off with a breathtaking start on Friday 18 April 2008. It was the greatest show in the cricketing world, changing the face of the game forever. By the time the match started on Friday, it was clear that IPL was changing cricket for all times to come. Every moment was a surprise. On the filed, arch-rivals left their countries behind and fought for their teams. Cheerleaders were specially flown from Washington to work the crowd's wild side.

This was also cricket's richest show ever. The moneymaking model of cricket had been tested before.

Here is another unique heading:

>   **Two Presidents**
>   **& their women**

An equally interesting heading to the same story:

>   **All the**
>   **Presidents'**
>   **women**

Heading or Headline Writing

These heading were used in a story that described the marriage of French President Nicholas Sarkozy who dumped his wife Cecillia and went all out for 41-year-old super-model-turned popsinger Carla Bruni, an Italian tyre heiress. The story came at the same time as the rumour of Vladimer Putin divorcing his 50-year-old wife Lyudmila to marry Olympic champion gymnast 24-year old Alina Kabayena, who was recently made a Member of Parliament.

Points to Remember

01. Punctuations, as far as possible, should not be the part of headings. Commas, dashes, exclamation marks and quotes do not look good in a headline.
02. Do not use stale jargon words.
03. An active verb should always be used, especially in functional headlines.
04. Do not fill too much information in the headline—you only have a few words to play with.
05. Avoid abbreviations. They look messy apart from being incomprehensible to some people.
06. Do not use 'he', 'she', or 'they.' Personalise wherever it is possible.
07. Readers should not be asked questions in headlines.
08. Avoid using the past tense in hard news headlines. It dates the story.
09. Avoid naming places unless they are a vital news element in themselves—as they often are in local newspapers.
10. The type size and width of the headline depends on the importance and the page on which it is to be used. The top story gets the maximum weight. The inside pages do not have big and wider headlines.

7

Writing the Introduction

Newspapers in the present day and time are voluminous. Many widely circulated newspapers contain 40 to 60 pages on week days. On Sundays the number of pages may be more than 100. With such a bulky and voluminous packet in hand containing more than 100 stories, editorials, lead articles (leaders) and news analyses, a reader becomes confused. The reason is that he may not be able to decide which stories to read and which to drop. The desk-editor has to pull the reader out of this dilemma. This is done by providing an introduction (called 'intro' in journalistic parlance) to every story, so that after reading just a few lines the reader can decide whether or not the story is of any interest.

As every human being has to have a neck that joins the head with the main body, every news story has to have an introduction that joins the headline or heading with the main body of the news. An interestingly, imaginatively and intelligently written intro attracts a reader to read the story. The main objective of the intro is to catch the attention of the newsreader when he is glancing through the pages. It is an invite to read the story. Therefore, it should indicate the central point of the story in the briefest possible form and be written in an interesting way.

Writing the Introduction

What is an Intro?

The first paragraph of a news story is known as the lead. Since it is the beginning of the story and also the briefest description of the story, it is the toughest part of the editing process. In many important newspapers the assignment of writing an intro is given to selected desk-editors who have complete command on language and specialise in condensed writing.

> **Points to look at when writing an intro**
>
> Tell only the main point of the story.
> Do not overplay the language or
> load it with unnecessary phrases,
> quotes or flowery language.
> You should only reveal what is the UNI—
> Unusual, Newsworthy and Interesting.

How to Write the Intro

One fundamental principal of writing an intro for a story is that it should not be the summary of the whole story. The objective of an intro is to highlight the story. The desk-editor's effort should be to arouse interest in the story so that the reader proceeds further and reads the full narrative Therefore, the desk-editor has to decide which from among the five Ws and one H—Who? Where? Why? When? What? and How?—forms the most important element of the story. It only should be revealed in the intro and not in the other questions. That is, while writing the intro, only one question out of the five Ws and one H should be revealed. Attempts should not be made to reveal other Ws and the H. If it is done the intro would lose its focus. One additional question may be selected only when it is essential to make the intro meaningful and interesting. The selection of a question out of the six to be answered in the intro should be based on the following three criteria:

- What is the **most interesting**?
- Which one is the **most newsworthy**?
- What is the **most unusual** part of the story?

Based on what comes out from the above, you have to decide on which is the question that is the most important in the story. Before making the final decision about the most important question, you should read the whole story carefully. Then you should try to find the following:

> What part of the story provides the most important information that can be called the unique point? In a way you have to *find out the central point* of the story.
>
> What was the main happening that made the story important? You have to *find out what happened* or what action was taken?
>
> What made the story newsworthy when the action was going on? You have to *find out the details of the happening or the action*.
>
> Which part of the story would most likely interest readers? You have to understand the interests of your readers and *find out what would interest your readers the most*.
>
> Is there *something unusual in the story*? If any thing has happened that has not taken place earlier it becomes the most significant element of the news and you write the intro around it.

Examples:

We give specimen intros that select the most important question, out of the six, for the following stories.

> **Who?** The suspected LeT operative Tariq Ahmad Dar, who was picked up by a Delhi Police team from Srinagar as a "crucial" link in the Delhi triple blast cases, isn't a product of *madarsa*.
>
> **How?** A 22-year pickpocket hit the bus passenger in the back of the head, then pulled a knife and stabbed him to death, the police said.
>
> **Where?** Hundreds of Naxalites struck in a big way tonight, raiding the police lines, police station and jail in the heart of Jehanabad in Bihar.

Writing the Introduction

Why? Her lawyers are expected to argue that Rita Singh has been the victim of disturbed relationships and influences since she was born.

When? Days after rescuers had given up hope of survivors, a baby trapped for seven days after the earthquake was pulled from the rubbles of a collapsed house in Muzaffarabad in Pak-occupied Kashmir.

What? An estimated 13 million Indian children were the victims of child abuse last year, the Ministry of Child Welfare report indicates.

Desk-editors, who are in the beginning of their career, commit a common mistake of trying to answer all the six questions in the intro. In that process they end up writing a complicated and confusing intro. Unfortunately, when some senior editor indicates this to them, they feel dejected, as they were not given proper training in intro writing in their journalism school. We give here an example of a confused and complicated lead:

Complicated leads that should not be used

Shyam Narayan, 22, of Greater Kailash-I was pronounced dead at AIIMS and his 20-year-old friend was hospitalised after a road accident at eight in the evening in which the truck that hit his scooter drove away.

The intro is confusing because it almost includes answers to all the six questions.

Who?—Shyam Narayan

How?—truck caused accident

Where?—AIIMS

Why?—road accident

When?—eight in the evening

What?—died because of road accident.

It is a hit-and-run story in which the truck hit two persons and drove away killing one person and injuring the other. This is a good human interest story of a young person dying in the prime of his youth because of reckless driving. It shows gross lack of sensitivity and social responsibility. The desk-editor should give a short crisp intro that should be the core of the story. The following intro is suggested. It answers only one question: What happened?

Edited intro that should be used

> Shyam Narayan, 22, died when a truck hit his scooter and drove away.

Identification Variations

A person should be identified in the intro if he is the key figure in the story. The identity of the person and what he does is important in a person-related story. A person's identification can be done in two ways. One is to identify the person in the first paragraph; however, it is not essential. Second, he may not be identified in the beginning but in subsequent paragraphs. The latter type can have two paragraphs in the intro. The incident is given in the first paragraph and the person related with the news in the second paragraph. The first description is known as immediate-identification and the second one as delayed-identification.

Immediate-identification: The subject of the story, the main person (it may also be the place or the central point) is identified in the intro. This method is used when the person mentioned or the major subject in the story is important or is well known. An example:

> Karishma Kapoor, the granddaughter of the famous star late Raj Kapoor, and Sanjay Kapur, the son of a well-known industrialist were married on Saturday. Both are childhood friends.

> Peter F. Drucker, the down-to-earth business thinker who defined the role of management guru, died on Friday at his home in Claremont, California. He was 95.

Delayed Identification: When the name of the main character in the story is not well known but what he has done or what happened to him was unique, the identification should be disclosed in the second paragraph. An example:

> A middle-aged person climbed the top floor of Vikas Minar in Indraprastha Estate, Delhi and threatened to commit suicide unless he was assured a job in the government.
>
> Ram Singh is an unemployed youth since his graduation fifteen years ago.

Blind intro: Many a times the desk-editor decides to make the story interesting by not revealing the identity of the main person or the central point of the story in the first paragraph. So he decides to write an intro that does not fall in either of the above two categories. He holds back the identity till the reader reaches the central point of the story. He, however, does not want to conceal the identity but only reveals it when he wants the reader to know it. This method of writing the intro, known as a 'blind intro' is good for incident- or research-related stories. An example:

> A study published today concludes that lactose intolerance is probably not responsible for bouts of intestinal disorder that people often blame on milk.

The story disputes the belief that intestinal disorders are caused by drinking milk. The story uses technical jargon 'lactose intolerance'. The intro does not explain the term. It also does not reveal the source of the study. The desk-editor teases the reader to read further and find out this information. So in the second paragraph he defines the 'lactose intolerance' and in the third paragraph identifies the source of the study.

It is essential that the desk-editor, before planning an intro, should fully understand the news story. If he does not do that he would not be able to write an effective intro. Once the focal point of the news is realised, the next effort should be to write the intro in a sharp, clear and understandable language. The reader should be able to understand in the minimum possible time what the news is all about.

Summary Leads

Intros can be written in different ways. Most of the desk-editors write it as the summary of the story. This is known as a direct intro because it gets right to the focal point of the story. Normally the lead should not be the summary of the story. But many a times, particularly if the story is long, the desk editor prefers to give a summary in the shortest possible length. This however is not common and should be avoided, except while writing articles.

An intro written in a summary style describes two aspects of the news story: First, what the central point of the story is, and second why the story is important. Most of the news stories in the daily newspapers have summary intros. Such intros are straightforward and contain only a single sentence. The one solitary sentence, however, must be complete and should observe all the normal rules of grammar, word usage, punctuation and verb tense. It should also include all the necessary articles—the words 'a', 'an' and 'the'. Proper tense should be used, for example if an event occurred in the past, the intro should not be written in the present tense. It should only be written in the past tense.

The intro should not be confused with the heading or the headline that describes the main element of the story in a few words. Only the key words are used and grammar rules or other conventions of the language are not followed. The shorter the heading, the better it is.

The intro, on the contrary, is the first, or at the most, two paragraphs of the news story.

An example:

Heading. Eight Tigers Go Missing

Intro: Tigers have vanished from the Ranthambhore National Park again, this time eight of them between August 2005 and October 2006.

The order of words in an intro should be: subject-verb-object. The intro should begin with the subject and then the object of the verb should be used. This order can be changed in an extraordinary intro. But it should only be an exception and not the general usage. This should be followed only when some unusual element of the story is to be highlighted.

The intro should be direct and clear. This is possible only when long introductory clauses are avoided. Such clauses cause confusion in the intro which then gets lost in other non-important details of the news. An example:

Intro as written:

> In the early hours of Saturday a petrol pump in Defence Colony was robbed by two persons after they took out a pistol and snatched the cash-bag containing about Rs. 50,000.

Intro as it should be written:

> Petrol pump robbed by two in Defence Colony Saturday morning.

If you closely analyse the intro as it was written, you will find that the key point of the news (robbery) is revealed only in the 14th word of the intro. The first 13 words that form the sentence are less important as far as intro to the news story is concerned. In the revised intro the key word or the action in the news is disclosed in the third word itself.

Technique to Write Effective Leads

Be Short

Every reader wants to know the news in the shortest possible time without making much effort to understand it. He also wants to get an overview of the news that familiarises him to the topic without getting involved in confusing details. Therefore, any lengthy intro of more than fifteen to twenty words would make it rambling, boring and harsh.

Writing a short intro is no easy task for a desk-editor but it is only a concise intro which would give intensity to a story.

An example

Intro as written:

Two persons robbed a shopper in a Gurgoan mall on Saturday. One boy distracted the shopper, and the second boy grabbed the wallet, that contained about 10,000 rupees.

The intro as it is written is superfluous. It reports that two persons robbed a person and narrates the robbery. The intro should not give details about the robbery. Only robbing of the persons should be described. The rest should be in the body of the news story. It should be edited as follows:

Intro as it should be written:

Two persons stole a wallet containing 10,000 rupees from a shopper in a Gurgoan mall on Saturday.

A two-sentence intro should be given only when the need is imperative. In a two-sentence intro the second sentence should emphasise the interesting or unusual fact of secondary importance.

An example: Polo playing is an important part of family life of the royal fa mily of Jaipur. Last year, Bhawani Singh and his cousin Jaswant won two matches in November and December.

After finishing the editing of the story the desk-editor should examine the intro critically to make sure that it is not tedious, boring and uneven and does not carry information that could be shifted to later paragraphs.

The desk-editor can shorten the intro by withholding the context that contains the background information. He can also withhold other details like dates, names and locations as they are not necessary. Names of the persons mentioned in the story should not be given in the intro. They should be given later in the main body of the story, as the readers may not be able to identify them in the lead. However, if the persons are well known, their names can be given in the intro, and that too if it is very necessary. Similarly, details like the precise time and location should be given in the later paragraphs and not in the intro. The story should be edited in such a way that the intro contains only the news peg or the focal point and not the minor details. If the intro contains minor details of the news, the main body would only be repeating the intro in some more detail.

A concise intro does not mean that it should contain only a few words, say five or six. An intro like 'Man robbed in Gurgoan mall' is more a heading than an intro.

Be Precise

A good intro should be exact, correct and should clearly specify the news peg. It should contain interesting details and should be precise so that the reader can generate an imagery of all that had happened. He should be able to visualise the event described in the story. The following intro aptly and creatively describes news in which a 19-year-old girl from a rich family was kidnapped at knifepoint.

Example:

She had never touched a knife—until someone held it to her chest.

The intro should not be abstract and uninteresting, full of ambiguous generalities. If the story is that the NDMC audit report for the fiscal year 2007–08 contained no objections and was passed without discussion, the following intro will be vague.

Intro as written:

> The NDMC has passed the all-clear audit report for the year 2007–08 without much discussion.

Intro as it should be written:

> NDMC, now in a healthy financial state, passes an all-clear audit report for 2007–08.

The desk-editors should avoid using stereotype phrases, ideas and expressions that have been too much in use and are now outdated. Old cliches are considered an ineffectual way of summarising a story. Do not use "a step has been taken" or that someone has moved "one step closer" to inform readers that a decision has been arrived at. It is better to be precise and that can be achieved by giving specific details.

Intro as written:

> A step has been taken toward banning hawkers in Connaught Place inner circle.

Intro as it should be written:

> The NDMC to ban hawkers in Connaught Place inner circle.

Uncertain and fickle intros should not be written, as they are not precise. Such intros are indistinct, too hypothetical, tentative and conditional. When writing an intro, the desk-editor should not indicate what would have happened if that had not happened. Only what has happened is important and should be written. The intro should contain only the most immediate and concrete detail.

Strong active verbs should be used

A verb is an essential part of a sentence, as no sentence can be complete without it. It is true for the intro also. Verbs, in fact, give a soul to an intro. A strong, specific, active and descriptive verb can enliven a dull lead. Strong verbs specify one specific action whereas weak verbs may cover a number of different actions. For example an intro like: *'The thief walked away with the cash'* is indistinct and insipid because it uses a weak verb. But edited to: *'The thief stole the cash'* is effective because it uses a distinct and expressive verb. The verb, besides being strong, should also be active. An active verb shows action and activity and a strong active verb does away with the need for adverbs and other modifiers that congest the intro and robs its competence.

Example:

> The speeding bus went through the closed level crossing,

Edited:

> Speeding bus tore through the level crossing.

The intro should also not use passive-voice formation. It means that the intro should not combine the past participle of a verb with some other form of the verb—such as *'is'*, *'are'*, *'was'* and *'were'*. A desk-editor can comfortably change a passive-voice intro into an active-voice intro. The method is simple. It can be done by changing the word order in the intro so that it narrates *'who-did-what'*.

For example:

> **The passive-voice intro:**
> Stones were thrown at the players in the cricket match.
>
> **Rewritten as an active-voice intro:**
> Spectators threw stones at the cricket players.

Highlight the Enormity of the News

Every story has some point or issue that needs to be emphasised. The desk-editor should try to find out that point or issue and highlight it in the intro. For example if there is a story on a plane crash, the emphasis in the intro should be on the number of lives lost and the damage caused in terms of cost, buildings or establishments or others. The following intro from a British newspaper shows how enormity can be highlighted in the intro to a story that described cops identifying the main suspect in the murder of Pakistan cricket coach Bob Woolmer from hotel security camera footage.

Intro:

> Cops identify the main suspect in Bob Woolmer murder case from hotel security camera.

Emphasise the Exceptional Bit in the News:

News usually is that which normally does not happen in day-to-day life. It is a deviation from the normal activity. When the news is of that nature, do emphasise the unusual in the intro. For example bank robberies are common in big cities and newspapers do not give much importance. But a robbery in the UTI Bank in Janakpuri (New Delhi) became a page-one story.

> A young man entered the Bank and went to the cabin of the Branch Manager.
>
> He was holding a round object in his hand. He told the Manager that it was a hand grenade. He demanded all the cash in the Bank. He also said there were two more persons in the Bank having bombs in their possession.
>
> He warned the manager not to inform the police after he left the Bank.
>
> He can do so after 15 minutes. The manager handed over the cash to him and informed the police only after 15 minutes. When he was caught he told the police that he was not having any bomb but was only having a ball rolled in strings in his hand.

A newspaper gave the following intro that was very apt.

Intro:

> A young boy robbed the UTI Bank with only a ball in his hand.

Use the Local Touch:

Readers first like to read those news stories that are related to their city, area or locality. They are always interested in news that concerns and affects their livelihood, lives and work and of those whom they know. If the news is not related to them or to their environment, they become less interested in it. However, an imaginative and creative desk-editor can localise news even from far away places by connecting it with some local or domestic interest. For example the Virginia Teck University shootout (a student moved from classroom to classroom and killed many students including two Indians) happened in Blacksburg, Virginia near Washington D.C. in the

Writing the Introduction

United States. The news would not have been of much interest in India as the early reports denied involvement of any Indian student. But when a newspaper wrote the following intro, it made the story relevant for India readers too.

Intro:

> At least 31 persons were killed in the deadliest shooting rampage in US history. No Indian students were injured in the attack when last news came in.

However, the next day it was reported that two Indians were killed. Though the story, a follow up of the previous day's story, focused on the rampage but the intro was as follows:

> An award-winning Indian professor and a 26-year-old student were among those killed in America's deadliest campus carnage.

Readers in India would not have developed any interest in the news as the scene of the occurrence was on the other side of the globe. But the imaginative desk-editor gave an Indian colour to it by connecting both the days' stories with India. This localisation made the story relevant for Indian readers.

An innovative desk-editor can localise the story (for example for Delhi readers) on using unfair means in the university examinations in India, without changing the substance and nature of story, by giving the following intro.

Lead as written:

> The UGC reported that the use of unfair means in Universities increased ten per cent during the last year.

Edited to give a local feeling:

> The use of unfair means in Delhi University last year increased six per cent against a national average of ten per cent, the UGC reported.

This is not a simple job. The desk-editor has to take extra pains to find relevant local information. In the above example the desk-editor made an extra effort to find out from the Controller of Examinations office the percentage of those using unfair means in the examination in Delhi University.

However, not all stories can be localised. If the story has no local angle, the desk-editor should give a simple and straightforward intro. The story should never be distorted arduously to give it a local angle.

Do not Advocate, Be Objective:

A news story is supposed to communicate information, facts and views to the readers. Therefore, the intro of a story should also be without comments and views. It should be objective. The desk-editor, like a reporter or correspondent, is not supposed to comment, interpret or advocate. If the desk-editor has an opinion he should not reflect it in the intro. It should be kept out of it and the story. A good desk-editor would avoid comments like "alert", "heroic" or "quick-thinking", or describing facts as "interesting" or "startling". Always state the obvious and be accurate. Example:

Intro as written:

> Speaking to the South Delhi Rotary Club, the General Manager of BSES discussed a topic of concern to all of us—the frequent power shedding in the area and assured regular power supply.

Intro as it should be written:

> The new General Manager of BSES assured south Delhi residents regular power supply.

The original intro was weak because it refered to "a topic of concern to all of us". The "us" should be identified because any topic cannot concern everybody.

Be Simple

An intro should be brief, clear, and simple. It is the first thing that is read immediately in the newspaper. If it is complex and

Writing the Introduction

difficult to understand, the reader would not waste time on the story whatever may be its relevance and importance. The following intro suffers from far too many details:

Intro as written:

> The citizens of Delhi are breathing sighs of relief following the announcement by the Chief Minister that the power distribution companies will be penalised if they shed power when it is surplus.

Intro as it should be written:

> Citizens of Delhi relieved, as the Chief Minister assures no power cuts.

Soft Intros

While summary intros are popular, as these are easy to write and understand, many creative desk-editors want to give different and interesting intros. These intros are also known as 'soft intros' and can be written in different ways. Nevertheless, these intros pick up the most interesting part of the story and begin with an amusing story, narration, quote or question. These intros are not of one sentence only but run into two to four sentences. Usually, after the first sentence, the second sentence describes the reason as to why the story is important. This sentence is known as the 'core sentence.'

Writing a soft intro is not easy and cannot be assigned to beginners. It requires creativity, imagination and a quick understanding of the story besides a strong knowledge base and wide reading experience. An example:

Summary Intro:

> The citizens of Delhi are breathing sighs of relief following the announcement by the Chief Minister that the power distribution companies will be penalised if they shed power when it is surplus.

Soft Intro:

> The Chief Minister of Delhi brings its citizens from darkness to light. In an announcement she promised that she would not allow power discos to shed power.

Soft intros were first used in the United States during the 1940s. *The Wall Street Journal* was the first newspaper to use a soft intro. Later other newspapers, particularly the *Los Angeles Times, The Miami Herald,* and *The Boston Globe* also gave freedom to their desk-editors to write alternate intros. These newspapers thought and believed that confining to summary intros restricted the editing creativity of the desk-editor and therefore they could not put in their best in editing a story. They also felt that the reader after reading the summary intro would know what the story was about and so would not like to read it further. Soft intros create an element of surprise in the story and different stories look different. Moreover, in the era of increasing competition from television , soft intros are like a breath of fresh air, as newspaper readers find something different in the story. A good editor, therefore, is not confined to writing only summery intros. He can write different types of intros and can select an appropriate type of lead for different stories. This breaks the monotony and a trend is set in the newspaper. However, writing different and flexible intros, needs special skills, intelligence, dexterity, imagination and creativity. Such intros, according to an American editor, are as "individual as writing, and writing is as individual as thinking." What is essential for writing alternate intros is a 'thinking-desk-editor'.

Soft intros have their critics as well. Many call them dangerous and others dub it as unprofessional because to them these are too literary. The conservative editors do not like long, windy and complicated intros. Long intros may make the reader disinterested in the story and he may stop reading it further. The reader, thus, may be denied the most important information and facts as they may be hidden in later paragraphs. Conservative editors want to give their readers simple and straight intros so that the readers have no difficulty in following the story.

Different Types of Soft Intros

01. Delayed or indirect intros: This is the most common category of a soft intro. Usually the intro begins with an intelligent opening sentence that often involves double meaning. It can also start with an interesting example or anecdote. The actual intro is in the second sentence that describes what the story is about. This is the reason this type of intro is known as an indirect or delayed intro.

The indirect intro can present an abstract or complex problem with an interesting joke or personal story so that every reader can associate herself or himself with the problem. The interesting example can develop an interest in the story.

Take for example the following story that may be appropriate for a soft intro.

> Reliance Fresh, the retail chain store from the Mukesh Ambani Reliance Group, decided to launch its own brand of tea, 'Reliance Tea'. The brand was launched to give a challenge to the existing brands—Lipton, Brook Bond and Tata. It was to be made available at all Reliance stores spread through out India, at a price quite less than the price of the existing brands. The Group thought that since Reliance was a strong brand and had the goodwill of the people, the tea would disappear from the shelves.

The body of the story further gives details of the share of each brand in the market and the total turnover of Reliance Fresh and how the Reliance Tea would affect the rival brands.

The indirect intro for the story:

> Reliance Fresh is likely to put the tea trade in a bind.
>
> he giant retailer is introducing its own brand called Reliance Tea.

The first sentence of the intro contains a jovial play on the word bind, though it indicates that the story concerns the tea business. The second sentence indicates what the story is all about. In place of this creative intro, the desk-editor could have given a simple summary intro as the following:

Conventional summary intro:

> Reliance Fresh is introducing its own tea brand called Reliance Tea. The tea will soon be on the shelves of the Reliance stores all over the country.

This intro is a simple one that tells what is going to happen in the tea business. Such an intro is easy to follow and is written under stress, when the deadline may be too close.

02. Multi-sentence intros: Some editors prefer the story-telling approach and want to narrate the intro in three to four sentences. They narrate a person, group, place or incident in which the situation typifies the story. After introducing the person, place or the incident, the main point of the story is given.

A multi-sentence intro:

The story:

> It is about a 12-year-old boy who was watching the TV. His sister, an infant and only three years old, was sleeping in the adjoining room. She got disturbed by the noise of the sound of the TV and started crying. The boy did not like to be distracted from watching his favourite programme. With a determination to silence her he got up from his couch and went to the girl. He scolded her and cajoled her to keep quiet. When she did not, he slapped her and directed her not to make any noise. She started crying more loudly. He coolly went to the bathroom, picked up the washing bat and hit her several times. She died on the spot. The boy came back, occupied his seat and started watching his favourite programme again.

This story appeared in the newspapers about ten yeas back. Some desk-editors gave the following intro:

Multi-sentence intro:

> Just twelve years of age, Shyam, Sam to many, was a chubby boy with curly hair. Fond of TV cartoon pragrammes, he never wanted to be disturbed while watching his favourite

Writing the Introduction 147

cartoon serials. But Friday night he was not a simple innocent boy. He turned into a criminal when he murdered his three-year-old sister. He was arrested and sent to a juvenile home by the court.

03. Intro to question-answer stories:

Sometimes stories, mainly interviews are written in the question-answer format. These stories focus on the views and experiences of one person. In such stories, the questions and answers are to be given as told by the interviewee. These, however, may be edited for length using the conventional guidelines and notations. These stories generally begin with an inverted pyramid-type intro that puts the important information first. Then they are given in the question-and-answer format.

The lead to such stories is actually at the beginning of the interview. It is normally given in italics. Sometimes it may be given in bold. The question-and-answer arrangement follows the inverted pyramid form and is in normal typeface.

Intro:

> The story of the turnaround of Indian Railways has become a case study for management schools across the world. From being a drain on the exchequer, the organisation today has generated profits. The new initiatives, especially the introduction of the Public Private Partnership (PPP) model, has helped the Railways to move into a brighter future. Indian Railways Finance Commissioner R Shivshankar spoke to this newspaper explaining future possibilities in the PPP model and strategies drawn to achieve the targeted growth.

04. Raising questions: Some desk-editors prefer to raise questions to make lively intros; though many do not like this style because they believe that news stories should not ask questions, rather they should answer them. Nevertheless, questions can make intros effective provided questions as intro are short, focused, intelligent, simple to understand and provoke the reader to think and react. Here is a question intro to a thought-provoking story.

The story:

> Eight students of Kendriya Vidyalaya, Rohini (Delhi), age between 10 and 14 years, were injured when a speeding Qualis rammed the Maruti van in which they were going to school. Two children fractured their collarbones; the remaining six received minor injuries. This was not the first accident involving small children going to school getting injured because of rash driving on roads. Last year two KV students died after a speeding Tata Sumo collided with their Maruti van.

Intro:

> Do you want your kid to be injured when going to school? But he may as the van can meet with an accident any day.

05. Enigmatic Intros

To arouse the readers' curiosity, an intro can be written to suggest some suspense or some suspicious development. There was a story in the newspapers towards the end of April 2007—three high ranking police officers were arrested in Gandhinagar (Gujarat) on a Supreme Court directive. Three Indian Police Service officers—one a Deputy Inspector-General and two Superintendents of Police—were involved in a fake encounter in which one person was killed. The three officers were charged with murder. They were called for recording their statements in the Gujarat police chief's office and were arrested to their utter bewilderment.

An enigmatic intro could be:

> The three IPS officers, when they left home, were sure to return, but didn't.

06. Unusual Intro: An intro can be curious and imaginative. A well-read desk-editor who wants to give a wider context to the story prefers to give an unusual intro. In a statement Lalu Prasad Yadav, the Union Railway Minister justified the imposition of Emergency in 1975 for curbing indiscipline in the country. He also said that if need arose, emergency could be imposed again. The stand taken by the Railway Minister was a bit awkward because he had been a severe critic of Emergency all through out. So much so that he named one of his daughters Misa, born during Emergency Misa (the law under which people were put behind the bars). A newspaper gave an unusual lead:

Unusual intro:

> Misa's father praises Emergency

Another example of unusual intro was a story of a blind pilot. Miles Hilton-Barber, a 50 year old blind British pilot flew more than 21,000 kilometres on Mach 7, 2007 from London to Sydney to raise funds to fight blindness in developing countries. He flew with a sighted co-pilot but relied on speech output from his navigation instruments to steer his course, and directed his plane from a wireless keyboard. The intro given by a newspaper was:

Intro:

> A blind pilot shows way to normal pilot flying more than 21,000
>
> kilometres to raise funds for blindness in developing countries.

07. Expressive Intro: Some stories need descriptive intros that illustrate the open picture of what happened. That is truer for war and police action stories. A newspaper published a story of an encounter between the Afghan forces and Taliban in Ghazni of Giro district in eastern Afghanistan. The battle began in the morning and till the end of the day the Taliban had an edge over the Afghan police. The latter retreated and the former thought that they had won. But in the morning the Afghan forces came with reinforcements from the Afghan national Army and the United States Coalition. The Taliban could not face such a strong contingent and ran away to take shelter in the adjoining districts. One newspaper gave an expressive intro that truly described the following story. The intro was:

Expressive Intro

> The sound of gun shots rings through the air, breaking the quiet of the evening. People scream as they run for shelter. Just outside the District Administrative Headquarters, the bodies of the District Head and the Police Chief lie in a pool of blood. But who has the last laugh?

Points to Remember

When writing an intro, remember the following points:
01. Be short and specific and not verbose and obscure.
02. Focus on the most unusual fact.
03. Focus on the most important aspect of the story.
04. Highlight the enormity of the news.
05. Form correct sentences. Use proper tense and necessary articles.
06. Be accurate and condensed.
07. An intro should contain only the main point of the story.
08. Form a simple sentence and not a long phrase.
09. Do not use passive-voice formation. Use strong active verbs.
10. Give a local touch to the news.
11. Do not give opinions in the intro.
12. When done, read the intro two to three times to make sure that all the above points have been taken care of.

Some examples of bad and good intros:

The story was on the One-Day International between India and Sri Lanka. It was to describe the significance of the match before the World Cup 2007 to be held in March. The intro was so complex and verbose that it failed to make any sense of the news peg.

> Kolkata: Their showdown at the Queen's Park Oval is still 44 days away. But for now, India and Sri Lanka are busy with a final stage rehearsal in a bid to fine-tune their acts. Clubbed in the same group in the World Cup, the two Asian neighbours couldn't have asked for a better opportunity to

size each other up than the four-match one-day series that gets under way at the Eden Gardens on Wednesday.

Another example of similar nature is a story on Virender Sehwag's poor performance in ODIs and his inclusion in the Kolkata match on 8 February 2007.

International matches are contests between two nations fighting for supremacy. It is the highest level of the sport. Hence it is not easy to accept the fact that international matches are sometimes reduced to becoming just selection matches—where the point of interests becomes certain individual performances and not really the teams and the result. That is what this India/Sri Lanka series is more about.

The following is an example of a simple and understandable intro. The story was on the inclusion of Manoj Tewari in the India team for the ODI between India and Sri Lanka on 8 Feb 2007 at Kolkata.

Kolkata: Manoj Tewari is enjoying the best week of his life. After a dream Ranji Trophy season where he amassed 796 runs at an average of 99-plus which helped him pick up the best batsman award on Tuesday evening, he has been rewarded with a surprise call-up to the Indian team.

Exercise

Write a soft intro to the following story:

A week after the arrest of Babulal Katara, officials of the Central Industrial Security Force (CISF) had to face the rage of a Union Minister when he was told to follow procedures as a regular passenger and undergo immigration and security checks. Denied privileges he is not entitled to, Minister of State for External Affairs Anand Sharma got into an ugly confrontation with CISF officials last week.

The CISF Director General, R. K. Das, has written to the Cabinet Secretariat, Home Ministry and Civil Aviation Ministry detailing the sequence of events. It has asked the authorities to "suitably inform" the minister that he does not fall in any of the categories accorded ceremonial facilities and exemption from pre-embarkation checks.

Sharma was to take the Air-India flight to London on the night of April 20. The MEA, which handles protocol at IGIA's ceremonial lounge, arranged for Sharma's access even though he is not officially entitled to use this facility. But the MEA claims that since he was on an official tour to attend an international Hindi conference in New York, the usual convention has been to extend this "courtesy", given that the protocol department comes under him.

The problem started when the CISF personnel posted there insisted that he undergo pre-embarkation-immigration and security checks just like any other passenger and reach the boarding gate through the normal channel.

Sharma is said to have insisted on using the special passage meant for VVIPs on the list of 23 persons/categories exempt from such checks. Frustrated by repeated denials, the DG's letter states the Minister "flew into a rage" and spoke to the CISF Director-General over the phone well past midnight.

The CISF letter claims that the door leading to the boarding area from the ceremonial lounge was opened for Lok Sabha Speaker Somnath Chatterjee, who was returning from Cyprus, and, at that moment, Sharma also walked through the gate "without a pre-embarkation security check". Left with no choice, the officials stamped his documents and delivered it to him at the boarding gate. Sharma's camp denies this.

They felt that it was "below the dignity" of the Minister to even comment on this matter. Sources close to Sharma feel that when he is accorded all the protocol in other countries during a visit, he should be entitled to the same here. As MoS in the MEA and who is in-charge of the protocol department, he should not be equated with any other minister, they argue.

Answer

Soft intro

The police blocked the door to the minister.

But he found his way, as every politician knows how to.

8

Understanding Language

An essential condition for becoming an efficient and an outstanding desk-editor is excellent writing skills. Besides an understanding of the basics of grammar and word usage, editors should become masters of language and expression. Desk-editors, who wish to become editors, should have an understanding of the following areas of good grammar.

Basic Sentence Structure

The structure of every sentence should be correct. A sentence must have three elements in it: a subject, a verb and a direct object.

The subject is the person or thing that is involved in action.

The verb describes the action.

The direct object is the person or thing acted upon.

Here is an example:

The thief killed the maid.

'The thief' is the person doing the action. It is the subject of the sentence. 'Killed' is the action and is the verb.

'The maid' is the person who was acted upon and is the direct object.

Sometimes the sentence also includes an indirect object. It indicates for or to whom an action was done. Here is an example:

> The thief killed the maid for money.

The verb can be transitive or intransitive.

The verb is called transitive when the verb denotes an action that passes over from the doer or subject to an object. In this sentence—*The police constable slapped the thief,*—the action denoted by the verb *slapped* passes over to an object, the *constable*. The verb *slapped* is, therefore, called a transitive (means passing over) verb.

The verb is intransitive when the action denoted by the verb stops with the doer or subject and is not passed over to an object. In this sentence—*The minister spoke emotionally*—the action denoted by *spoke* stops with the minister and does not pass over to any object. The verb *spoke* is, therefore, called an intransitive (means not passing over) verb.

Verbs are used either in a transitive or an intransitive form. But many verbs can be used in both ways. In the sentence— *The team leader flies the flag*—the verb *flies* is used in a transitive sense; the action is transferred to the *flag*, which is the direct object. But in the following sentence: *The flag flies from the King's palace*, the verb *flies* is used in an intransitive form; the verb merely describes the action of the subject.

A complete sentence, therefore, needs at least a subject and a verb. The subject may be implied or understood, as in a command such as *go!* Sentences may also need direct or indirect subjects, depending on whether the verb is transitive.

The editor can embellish a simple sentence in a number of ways. One may combine two independent clauses—the clause that could stand alone—to make a compound sentence.

> Reading is the minister's favourite hobby,
> but he enjoys golf too.

The alternative is to combine an independent clause with a dependent one to make a complex sentence. Dependent clauses are introduced by a subordinating conjunction, which makes the clauses incapable of standing alone.

Subordinating conjunctions are words and phrases like *because, as a result of, after, before, whenever* or *as long as*.

The minister's wife listens to his speech whenever the minister speaks in a public function.

Sentences may also contain phrases, which are related groups of words that lack a subject and verb; prepositional phrases and verb phrases are common types. They may be incorporated in the body of the sentence or may introduce the main clause. The first of the following two sentences ends with a prepositional phrase and the second begins with a verbal phrase.

- People in Delhi spend more time at India Gate during the summer evenings.
- Tired after a long speech on Independence Day, the Prime Minister took a nap.

Sentence parts can be combined and arranged in many ways. Varying sentence structures can keep one's writing from becoming too predictable and simplistic, but simple sentences that stick to subject-verb-object order are the clearest and most easily understood.

Active and Passive Voice

Sentences that use the subject-verb-object order are active voice sentences. A passive voice sentence turns that order around. The direct object of the active voice sentence becomes the subject of the passive voice sentence; the subject becomes part of a prepositional phrase or disappears altogether, and the verb is replaced with its past participle and some form of the verb 'to be.' When converted to the passive voice, the sentence: *The thief killed the maid.* would look like this:

The maid was killed by the thief.

It can be said that a verb is in the active voice when its form shows that the person or the thing denoted by the subject does something. In other words, the subject is the doer of the action. The active-voice is so called because the person denoted by the subject acts or is active.

In passive voice sentences, the verb shows that something is being done to the person or thing denoted by the subject. The passive voice is so called because the person or thing denoted by the subject is not active but passive; that is, it suffers or receives some action.

In brief, voice is that form of a verb that shows whether what is denoted by the subject does something or has something done to it. We give here a few examples in which the active voice is changed to passive voice.

Active Voice	Passive Voice
Sita loves Savitri.	Savitri is loved by Sita
The mason is building the wall.	The wall is being built by the mason.
He will finish the work in a fortnight.	The work will be finished by him in a fortnight.
Why did your brother write such a letter?	Why was such a letter written by your brother?

It should be clear that when the verb is changed from the active to the passive voice, the object of the transitive verb in the active voice becomes the subject of the verb in the passive voice. (In the first sentence, Savitri is the subject of the object of 'loves' in the active voice. But when it is converted to passive voice, Savitri becomes the subject of 'is loved' in the passive voice.)

Since the object of a verb in the active voice becomes the subject of the passive form, it is essential that only a transitive verb be used in the passive voice, because an intransitive verb has no object.

The desk-editor should know when to use the active voice and when to use the passive voice.

The active voice is used when the agent (doer of the action) is to be made prominent. The passive voice should be used when the person or thing acted upon is to be made noticeable. The passive is, therefore, generally preferred when the active form would involve the use of an indefinite or vague pronoun or noun (somebody, they, people, we and so on.) as subject.

For example:

The car of the businessman was stolen.
(Someone has stolen the car of the businessman.)

The minister was asked his name.
(They asked the minister his name.)

English is spoken all over the world.
(People speak English all over the world.)

The minister has been invited by the students.
(The students have invited the minister.)

The ministry will execute all orders promptly.
(All orders will be executed promptly.)

In such cases the agent with *by* is usually avoided.

Another fact to be kept in mind by desk-editors is that the passive voice sentences are usually longer than active voice sentences, though they say the same thing. Those extra words are wasted words and are stumbling blocks for readers. Also to be noted is that in a passive voice sentence the main character may disappear. In some cases, the identity of the main character is clear from the context.

In other cases, the passive voice disguises responsibility. If a disaster strikes or someone is injured by a defective product, then the government officials or business managers may admit *'mistakes were made,'* but notice that the passive construction reveals nothing about who made the mistakes or why. The passive voice is the defender of all who seek to evade responsibility. It is the antagonist of all who seek clarity.

Agreement

A common mistake that desk-editors make is when they do not make nouns, pronouns and verbs agree with each other.

The three are either singular or plural and should be in agreement with each other. Nouns and pronouns, besides being singular or plural, also indicate gender—masculine, feminine or neutral. When working on a copy, it should be ensured that the nouns, pronouns and verbs agree with each other. An important point that should always be kept in mind is that a singular subject should have a singular verb, and a plural noun should have plural pronouns. This principle is basic to editing and simple to follow.

Subjects and Verbs

The verb in a sentence must agree with the subject in number and person. The general principles to follow are:

1. If the subject of a sentence is singular, use a singular verb; and if the subject is plural, use a plural verb. For example:

The police arrested Shyam and Anil on robbery charges.

2. If two singular nouns refer to the same person or thing, the verb should be singular. For example:

With the death of Nehru, the country lost a great statesman and political leader.

3. If two subjects together express *one idea*, the verb used can be singular. For example:

Fruit and milk is the only food that Morarji Desai took.

4. If *each* or *every* is used in the sentence, the verb should ordinarily precede the singular subject. For example:

Every man, woman and child was celebrating the Indian victory over Australia in the tri-final series in 2008.

Each day and each week brings a new life to the college.

5. Two or more singular subjects connected by *or, nor, either...or, neither...nor* should use a verb that is singular. For example:

No nook or corner of the rock where the murder took place was left unexplored.

Neither he nor his wife was there.

Either the driver or the maid has stolen the money.

6. When the subjects joined by *or* and *nor* are of a different number, the verb should be plural and the plural subject should be placed next to the verb. For example:

Shyam or his friends have beaten the boy.
Neither Shyam nor his friends were hurt in the fight.

7. When the subjects joined by *or* and *nor* are different in person, the verb should agree in person with the one nearest to it. Such as:

Either he or I am mistaken.
Neither you nor he is to be blamed.

8. When subjects differing in person are connected by *and*, the verb should always be in the plural. For example:

Shyam and I are going to attend the programme.

9. Some nouns may appear to be plural because they end with 's'. In fact, they are not plural but singular. Examples are 'economics', 'politics' and 'physics.' These should be edited as:

Economics is an essential discipline in the B.A. Programme of the University of Delhi.

10. Some nouns are known as collective nouns. These nouns are those that refer to groups or collections of individuals as a whole. Some such words are: 'committee', 'club', 'jury', 'regiment', 'team', etc. Proper nouns that identify organisations are also collective names. Examples are: 'Rajya Sabha', 'Congress', 'Tata', etc. Usually collective nouns are considered singular and require singular verbs and pronouns. Examples are:

The Editors Guild of India has begun a programme to help journalists improve their writing skills.

11. Some collective nouns are sometimes confusing because they end with 's', but take a singular verb. An example is:

A few thousands is a good crowd for a political rally in Delhi.
Ten rupees is a high price for a cup of tea.

12. Collective nouns mentioned above cause the most problem with noun-pronoun agreement. Most desk-editors are not sure

whether a collective noun is singular or plural. They write it both ways, using singular verbs with collective nouns but use plural pronouns to take their place. For example:

Tata Motors is launching their one-lakh rupees car, Nano, next year.

The Indian cricket team won their second victory in a row in Australia in the tri-final series.

13. The above principle does not apply if a collective noun is used in a plural sense. In such a situation the plural pronoun is needed. An example:

The GOI committees for Commonwealth Olympics reviewed their targets for the completion of various projects.

14. When a plural noun is used between a singular subject and its verb, the verb is often wrongly made to agree with the nearest plural noun instead of with the real subject. Such mistakes should be carefully avoided. Some examples of how to edit such sentences are:

None of the students in the group is intelligent.

Neither of the bodyguards of the President is short in stature.

Each of these minerals is found in India.

A variety of pleasing objects charms the foreign tourists in India.

Japan importers complained that the quality of mangoes exported from India was not good.

15. Words joined to a singular subject by 'with', 'together with', 'in addition to', or 'as well as', are parenthetical, and therefore do not affect the number of the verb. Examples are:

The head of the police station in Jharkhand, along with his men, was massacred.

The President of the United States, with his entourage, has arrived at the Rashtrapati Bhawan.

The father, as well as the mother and the child, likes hot chocolate.

Understanding Language

16. The verb 'to be' takes the same case after it as before it. Example:

I knew that boy to be him.

17. When the subject of the verb is a relative pronoun, care should be taken to see that the verb agrees in number and person with the antecedent of the relative. An example:

The city counselor said, "I, who am your friend, will protect your interests."

Every one believes that his is one of the best mothers that have ever lived.

18. Pronouns should be handled with care because they can lead to ambiguity. Too many pronouns within one sentence or paragraph can perplex readers. Take this example: "The finance committee presented its recommendations to the Board. It discussed it before returning it for further considerations." If carefully edited, the desk-editor will limit the use of pronouns to make sure that each one has a clear antecedent. It could be rewritten in the following way:

The finance committee presented its recommendations to the Board, which revised it and returned the recommendations to the committee for further consideration.

19. Modifiers are words or phrases that limit, restrict or qualify some other word or phrase. Modifiers should appear as close as possible to the word or phrase they modify. Misplaced modifiers can make sentences ambiguous and confusing. "He narrated the tribulation of being held hostage with tears running down his cheeks" is an example of the misplaced modifier. It should be edited in the following way:

He narrated, with tears running down his cheeks, the tribulation of being held hostage.

Or

With tears running down his cheeks, he narrated the tribulation of being held hostage.

In the unedited sentence, the phrase "with tears running down his cheeks" follows 'hostage', and readers might think that the phrase modifies the word 'hostage'. But, in fact, the phrase really describes how the person behaved as he talked about his tribulation. The word that the phrase modifies is, 'narrated'.

20. Modifiers hang when the word or phrase they are supposed to modify does not appear in the sentence. It may happen when a thoughtless or hurried reporter begins the sentence intending to describe an idea one way and then switches mid-sentence to express it in another way. For example, the reporter may write: "Pleased with everyone's success, the regiment received congratulations from the commandant." This could be edited in the following way:

Pleased with everyone's success, the commandant congratulated the regiment.

Readers of newspapers have the habit of understanding introductory words and phrases to modify the subject of the sentence. If that is not the case, the modifiers are either misplaced or dangling.

21. Inanimate subjects or concepts should not be treated as human beings. Objects like houses, scooters, shops and plants cannot hear, think, feel or talk. But more often than not they are treated as persons. This mistake is so common and is repeated more often that readers become used to it. They personify such words like nations, companies and machines. For example:

Max Hospital treated the minister for heart attack.

The blue line bus driving on the Ring Road slammed on its brakes when a two-wheeler suddenly came in front of it.

The above expressions are wrong because a hospital cannot treat a patient. Only the doctors in the hospital can do this job. Similarly the bus cannot slam its brakes, only its driver can.

Personification must be avoided when editing a story or an article. The reason is that a story in a newspaper should have credibility. The credibility is established if the incident or statement is attributed to a person and not to an organisation, city or institution. Also, persons cannot be held responsible for their actions if it is attributed to an organisation.

Common Errors and Unsuitable Words

Editing is an art and requires correct understanding of the language and words. The desk-editor should know which word to use for which situation. Reporters and correspondents write in great hurry and therefore are unable to think of correct and appropriate words. It is the job of the desk-editor to correct the copy and ensure that appropriate words and expressions are used. We give here some of the most common writing mistakes made by reporters and corespondents that should be corrected by desk-editors.

Punctuation

1. *Apostrophes should not be used in possessive pronouns.* Possessive pronouns depart from the usual rules about possessives and are never followed by an apostrophe; 's' is to be used in place of an apostrophe. Something can be 'yours', 'hers', 'its' or 'theirs' and not *your's, her's, it's,* or *their's.*

If it is written: The car is their's, but it's interior is not pleasing.

It should be corrected to: The car is theirs, but its interior is not pleasing.

2. *Put commas inside or outside the quotation marks as per the language style the newspaper follows.* If the newspaper follows the American pattern, the commas and periods (full stops) should always be inside the quotation marks. They also go inside single quotations. If single and double quotation marks appear together, give a space between the two. On the contrary, in the British style, the commas and period go outside the quotation marks. They also go outside the single quotations. In this situation the quotation mark precedes the period. You should not mix the two styles. Carefully observe the difference between the two:

American Style: "The Americans while writing use commas inside the quotation marks," said the teacher to the class. "They also go inside single quotations, which to many may 'seem to be unnatural.' "

British style: "The British when they write use commas outside the quotation marks", said the teacher to the class. "They also go outside single quotations, which to many may 'seem to be unnatural'."

3. *Capitalise on your use of colons.* The first word to be used after a colon should be capitalised only if it is a proper noun or is the beginning of a new sentence. Use lower case if the first word after the colon only introduces a list or is a sentence fragment. For example:

Incorrect: The desk-editor should know it fully: the first word of a complete sentence after a colon is to be capitalised.

Correct: The desk-editor should know it fully: The first word of a complete sentence after a colon is to be capitalised.

Incorrect: The desk-editor should understand this: Proper punctuation.

Correct: The desk-editor should be sure to understand this: proper punctuation.

4. *Use hyphens only when required.* Before using a hyphen you should be clear whether something is a compound word, two words or hyphenated. Many a times the concept can be expressed in more than one way, depending on its place in the sentence. Here are a few examples:

- How to use: back yard, backyard, or back-yard?

If used as a *noun* it should be back yard. Example: The thief entered from the *back yard*.

If used as an *adjective*, it is to be used as one word. Example: The monkey sat on the *backyard* pillar of the minister's bungalow.

It is not to be used as back-yard.

- How to use: Full time, fulltime, or full-time?

It is hyphenated when used as an *adjective*: He is a *full-time* director in the company.

It is two words when used as an *adverb*: He works *full time* as a director in the company.

It is not to be used as fulltime

- How to use: Fund raiser, fundraiser or fund-raiser?

It is two words when used as a noun to specify the function of raising money: *Fund raising* in the coming general election would be challenging for every political party.

When used as a noun to describe an event or someone who raises money, it is to be hyphenated as: The new party is looking for a new *fund-raiser*, and it might appoint a professional to raise maximum funds.

It is also hyphenated when used as an adjective. Example: The *fund-raising* campaign of the Bharatiya Samta Party was a grand success in the last elections in Uttar Pradesh.

- How to use: Makeup, make up or make-up?

It is one word when used as a *noun* or *adjective*. Example: Anu, the known nutritionist, put on her best *makeup* before appearing in the *makeup* examination about the nutritional *makeup* of common foods.

When used as a *verb*, it is two words. An example is: Anu knew it well that she needed to *make up* the examination.

- How to use: Teenage, teen age or teen-age?

It is to be always hyphenated whether used as a *noun* or *adjective*.

Example: T*een-age* children develop emotional problems when they reach that age.

Singular/Plural

A single unit that is composed of many people is a singular word like 'a team', 'a newspaper', 'a college', 'a group', or 'an organisation'. Such words should use singular possessive pronouns such as 'it'.

> *Wrong use:* The Indian team won *their* first match in the tri-final series with Australia.
>
> The Editors Guild of India had *their* annual general meeting yesterday.
>
> The Hindu College of the University of Delhi will hold *their* annual day function tomorrow.
>
> *Correct use:* The Indian team won *its* first match in the tri-final series with Australia.

The Editors Guild of India had *its* annual general meeting yesterday.

The Hindu College of the University of Delhi will hold *its* annual day function tomorrow.

The expressions *here's* and *there's* are inconsistent. These words mean 'here is' and 'there is'. These words should be used only if you are pointing out a single item. Otherwise, use 'here is' and 'there are'. It would not be incorrect if you use I and I. But such usage is inept reading.

Wrong use: *Here's* the minutes of the meeting. *There's* the full details of the discussion.

Correct use: *Here is* the minutes of the meeting. *There are* the full details of the discussion.

Adverbs and Adjectives

Multiple-word modifiers should be hyphenated. Two or more words that express a single concept as an adjective before a noun are known as multiple-word modifiers. These should always be hyphenated. Some examples are:

Wrong use: Just because Sharma had a *better than average* bowling score does not mean he should act like a know it all.

A well *qualified engineer* was competing for a full time job with a foreign qualified person.

Still boiling water spilled over the child causing severe injuries.

Correct use: Just because Sharma had a *better-than-average* bowling score does not mean he should act like a *know-it-all*.

A *well-qualified* engineer was competing for a *full-time* job with a foreign qualified person.

Still-boiling water spilled over the child causing severe injuries.

However, there are a few exceptions to this rule. If the first word ends in '-ly', the word is not to be hyphenated. Adverbs ending in '-ly' are also not be hyphenated with the adjectives they modify. By adding the '-ly' suffix, you create a word that automatically modifies the word that follows it. Two examples are:

Wrong use: When she entered the room she had a *purely-harmless* motive.

The *badly-damaged* car that hit the tree was fully insured.

Correct use: When she entered the room she had a *purely harmless* motive.

The *badly damaged* car that hit the tree was fully insured.

Clauses

When who, which or that should be used: The sentence should start with 'who' or 'whom' if it has a clause about a person or animal, say a dog, which has a name. Whenever you include a clause in a sentence that talks about a person and animals that have names, the clause should start with 'who' or 'whom'.

Wrong use: The man *that* was at the scene of the accident refused to talk to the police.

The police dog, Jenny, *which* was brought to the site of the theft, was unable to reach the robber.

Correct use: The man *who* was at the scene of the accident refused to talk to the police.

The police dog, Jenny, *who* was brought to the site of the theft, was unable to reach the robber.

Reporters are in the habit of frequently using the word 'which' when 'that' should be used. Therefore the desk-editors should be clear in their minds about the use of these two words. Remember, if it is a clause that is essential to the sentence, do not begin the sentence with the word 'which'. Clauses that cannot be eliminated without changing the meaning of the sentence should begin with the word 'that', and not 'which'. The latter should be used only for nonessential clauses or to begin a clause within a clause.

Wrong use: The owner of the shop had pasted the sign, *which* announced the closing of the shop at the main door.

The owner of the shop felt that the sign *that* was on the main door was not visible from the road.

Correct use: The owner of the shop had pasted the sign *that* announced the closing of the shop at the main door.

The owner of the shop felt that the sign, *which* was on the main door, was not visible from the road.

Whenever you read a sentence with the word 'that', ask yourself if you can delete the word 'that' and still achieve clarity. If so, delete it.

Capitalisation

In journalistic writings, fewer words are capitalised than in academic writings. In general, nouns are not capitalised unless they refer to formal organisations, proper geographic names or official job titles (but only when used before a person's name). It is also important to use capital letters for words that are trademarked names like Tata and Mother Dairy. For example, 'Economics classes' should be written as 'economics classes' and 'Indian economics' as 'Indian Economics'. 'Director' of an institute is written as 'director'.

Clarity

In newspaper writing, clarity is the first virtue. The reader scans through the newspaper in great hurry and does not have the time and patience to go though ambiguous sentences. For example read the following sentence:

> The information released by the National Council for Education Research and Training show that the failure rate at one school soared from three per cent to around 20 per cent *since* trainees this year *have* had to take the test on a computer rather than with a pen and paper.

In this sentence the confusion is, does *'since'* mean *'because'* or *'after'*?

Readers would be able to understand the news fast and clearly if the desk-editor **substitutes** *'since'* with *'after'* and **deletes** *'have'* and *'around'*.

Do not use 'one' and 'you' in the same sentence. It is all right when you are in conversation with your friend. But when you are editing a news story you cannot do that. For example:

> And surely *one has* to be a strong personality to have a prospering business, while raising a family.

The expression becomes clearer if you edit it the following way:

> And surely you have to be a strong personality to have a prospering business, while raising a family.

'Only' is a complex word to use. It should not be used frequently. For example:

> The professor had *only* moved from Mumbai to Delhi last year because his wife needed treatment at AIIMS.

Does the story indicate that the professor came to Delhi recently or that he came because his wife needed treatment that was available only at AIIMS? In a news story neither point should be emphasised. The facts should speak for themselves. Therefore, the story would be clearer if 'only' is deleted.

Most of the desk-editors confuse the use of 'who' and 'whom'. "Who did you invite?' is not the correct use of the language. But it has come to stay in mainstream journalism. But using 'whom' for 'who' or 'us' for 'we' is not correct. For example, in the following sentence 'who' should be used in place of 'whom'.

> It is easier to establish friendship with a person *whom* the polls suggest would not win.

Punctuation

The desk-editor should be well versed in the use of punctuation. Most of the desk-editors do not consider that punctuation does play an important role in a sentence. Here are a few common mistakes that are committed by desk-editors.

1. An essential apostrophe is left out in the following sentence: '*Its no use complaining*'; the apostrophe should be used in 'its'. (It's is a contraction for 'it is' and 'its' is possessive. Apostrophes are not used in possessive pronouns.)

2. Use an apostrophe carefully. Example: 'Apostrophe's are difficult to use'; here the apostrophe is not to be used.

3. Do not put an apostrophe in the wrong place. Example: 'Nehru was the peoples leader', apostrophe should be used in 'peoples'. It should be *people's*.

4. Do not leave out an essential hyphen. Example: 'He is a tourist cab chauffeur' there should be hyphen between 'tourist' and 'cab'. It should be 'tourist-cab'. It can also be rewritten as: 'He drives a tourist cab'.

5. Do not put in an unnecessary hyphen. Example: 'It is a commonly-observed phenomenon'; a hyphen is not needed between 'commonly' and 'observed'. It should merely be 'commonly observed'.

6. Do not put a hyphen in the wrong place. Example: 'The crowd was a hot dog- munching cricket fan'; a hyphen is not needed, as 'hotdog' is one word. It should be edited as: 'The crowd was a hotdog munching cricket fan'.

7. Do not put more than two dashes in one sentence. Example: 'He went to Meerut—by bus—how else?—to attend the marriage of his friend'; the first dash should not used. It should be: 'He went to Meerut, by bus—how else?—to attend the marriage of his friend'.

8. Use a question mark after a rhetorical question. Example: 'Have you ever thought of moving to Mumbai'; use a question mark (?) at the end of the sentence in place of a period (.).

9. In a descriptive phrase, use a second comma. Example: 'Saurav Ganguli belongs to Kolkata, West Bengal and plays cricket'; a comma (,) should be used after West Bengal too.

10. Do not put quotation marks ("...") with slang. Example: Most of the novae rich persons are "yuppie"; quotation marks should not be used.

Understanding Language

The following story, published in the Sunday edition of a Delhi-based multi-edition national newspaper has certain language mistakes. Read the story carefully and point out the mistakes:

> The 34-year-old god-woman endowed with all the physical assets to make it big in the art of the First Sin, sits on a wooden plaque on the floor wearing nothing but a gossamer robe in rich lighting and surrounded by several men, including her first husband, his brother, who is also her present husband, his son and trusted women.
>
> The helper showers her first with water and milk, creating quite a sight for the men as water and milk flow down the most pleasurable troughs of her body. The scene then cuts to an ashram, tucked away in a sparsely populated rural nook. The woman is now clad in rich white robes, replete with a turban.
>
> The septuagenarian former Union Minister, who is waiting for orders from the Mata or Thaya, walks away with a *diya* in his hands to a corner at her command.
>
> Every scene is video-graphed and the CD is available to those who have money or power and those who will to be the Mata's servile disciples. The god-woman was a simple cinderwinch of a female body some years ago, before her present incarnation.

The story is badly edited. The sentences are long, incomplete and wrongly formed. Appropriate words have not been used. It should be rewritten in the following way:

> The 34-year-old god-woman is sitting on a wooden plaque on the floor. She, gifted with all that makes a woman attractive, is seductive. Wearing nothing but a see-through gown, the bright lighting would fascinate any beau for the First Sin. Several men who surround her include her former husband and his brother, who is her present husband and his son. A group of trusted women are also a part of the crowd.
>
> An attendant enters to give her a shower, first with water and then milk. As water and milk flow down her curvaceous body, a sensuous atmosphere, particularly for the males, is created.

The arena now shifts to an ashram that is situated in a sparsely populated rural corner where a septuagenarian former Union Minister waits for her. The same god-woman, *Mata* or *Thaya*, wearing a turban and an opulent white dress, orders him to move to a corner. He moves towards the directed space.

The entire episode is videotaped. The CD is available to all those who can afford the price or are powerful. They are all *Mata*'s cringing devotees. A few years ago, before her present incarnation, the god-woman was a simple Cinderella, an ordinary dame.

9

Layout and Design

Newspapers are brought out in different sizes. However, two sizes are most popular: broadsheet and tabloid. Broadsheet is also known as 'text-size' and tabloid 'half size'. *The Times of India, Hindustan Times, The Hindu, The Indian Express, Navbharat Times* and hundreds of others are all broadsheet newspapers. The size of the broadsheet has been changing over the years. In India these days it is 35cm x 55cm in size. In the past it used to be slightly larger in breadth and length.

Mid-Day, The Afternoon Courier and many others are published in the tabloid size. The tabloid size is approximately half of the broadsheet. At present in India it is sized at 28 cm x 35 cm. Many other newspapers have developed a unique size of their own. *Mint*, the business newspaper from the Hindustan Times Group is 27 cm x 42 cm in size. *Mail Today* is 32 cm x 47 cm in size. These are known as 'compact' sizes.

The size of the newspapers in India has been changing because of business reasons. A few years back the size of the broadsheet was shortened by Hindustan Times to reduce the cost of newsprint. Nevertheless, it also wanted to give a different look to its newspaper so that it could have an edge over its competitors. Other newspapers followed suit and changed their sizes as it also reduced their costs of production.

Tabloids also chose different sizes to give their paper a unique appearance.

There is no historical significance in the selection of the size for a newspaper. But over centuries a broadsheet has become associated with serious journalism and is considered respectable. It is also the size that is selected by mainstream and national newspapers. On the other hand, a tabloid is considered to be a non-serious paper, mainly gossip and full of soft stories. It also makes extensive use of pictures, strip cartoons, etc. News is presented in concentrated form that can be easily understood. Till a few years back serious newspapers were not in the tabloid form as these were considered flimsy and lacking solidity. But now that notion has been dropped because the size is easier to manage and hold, especially for people hurrying to work and using public transport. Many newspapers have adopted a tabloid size, for example *Mail Today*.

The tabloid size is also being preferred because of many other reasons. First, it provides bold poster-style layout that was introduced for the first time by the *Daily Mirror* from London. Other newspapers followed it in the United Kingdom and later throughout the world. Secondly, it makes it possible to accept cheaper full-page advertisements and more regular solus (single) positions. The advertisers prefer it because the full page in a broadsheet would be many times expensive. To the newspapers it means more advertising revenue and better economics. However, despite these advantages, most quality newspapers throughout the world have not shifted to tabloid. They still prefer broadsheet because the longer text of news and features are better accommodated in broadsheet. *The Times of India* and *The Hindu* from India, *Financial Times* from Britain, *The New York Times* from the United States, *The Dawn* from Pakistan, and the international newspaper *The International Herald Tribune* have retained their traditional broadsheet shape. However, it can be mentioned here that *Le Monde* in France is a quality tabloid.

Local and evening newspapers, more often than not, prefer tabloid size. The reason may be that they have lesser number of pages and a broadsheet of four pages would look flimsy. But the same, when converted into tabloid would be of eight pages and would look graceful. In recent years even the morning papers have begun to consider tabloid size for their morning editions. In early 2008 when the India Today Group of publications decided to bring out a daily morning paper it opted for a tabloid size. Nevertheless, it did not opt for the traditional size of tabloid. It brought out *Mail Today* in a 32 cm x 47 cm size, which is neither broadsheet nor tabloid. It is known as the 'compact' size.

Well-read readers prefer to read a broadsheet newspaper, as they are interested in reading lengthy articles. The reason is that they have been educated to use the printed word as a principal means of communication. Moreover, 'cutouts' have better impact and pictures can be blown to bigger sizes in broadsheets to give better impact. A tabloid is meant for readers who prefer light reading, and want to get their information from visual impressions and do not want to read a lot of text. The editors of tabloids, therefore, give more space to headings and pictures than the body text. The intention is to tell the story at a glance. The tabloid editors give big-letter bold headlines to indicate, 'This is important!' or 'This is interesting!'

Designing a Newspaper

A newspaper is a collection of news, news analyses, features, editorials, lead articles, pictures, cartoons and the most important, at least from the revenue point of view, the advertisements. All these ingredients have to be put together in a planned and coordinated way so that the newspaper not only looks attractive but is also interesting to read. This process is known as 'visual design'. Moreover, the reader should be able to locate easily, the news and features of his choice without wasting time in searching them. So there has to be a method in planning and designing a newspaper. Various news, features, lead articles, news analyses, editorials, pictures, cartoons and advertisements are not just dropped into the various pages. These have to be properly placed and organised which requires a well-thought planning. Also, colours have to be used according to a pattern; the designer should not just use them without any purpose. In fact, newspapers today spend a fabulous amount of money to get the newspaper designed by design specialists—the best one of international repute charging a small fortune.

The most reputed newspaper designer of the contemporary world is Mario R Garcia, the American newspaper designer. He has designed *The Hindu, Mint, Mid Day, Malayala Manorama, Hindustan Times, Sakal Times, Business Line, The Week, Sportstar,* and *India & Global Affairs.* Garcia is from Cuba and is based in Tampa, Florida.

The concept of the design of a newspaper has to be conceptualised by the editor. He has to visualise the entire newspaper and should have a strong say in the final design of the newspaper. It is because everything goes under the name of the editor. Therefore, he has to have an overall editorial plan or design of the newspaper in his mind. It would be the description of the editorial philosophy and policy. It would indicate different news departments, columns and other features. This is to be discussed with various managers in circulation and advertisement to gauge the market reaction to the design. After all the newspaper is to be sold in the market and if the readers' reaction is not favourable the newspaper would become a 'file newspaper'—a newspaper that is not read but only filed in offices for record purposes.

The Times of India, several years back, conceptualised a weekly supplement as an add-on to its daily newspaper. When the dummy was prepared editors and managers in the circulation and advertisement departments discussed it. There were sharp differences between the editors and managers. Ultimately the design went to the Managing Director, who was also the owner of the newspaper. He suggested that a few copies of the dummy be taken to various points in Connaught Place and shown to passers-by for their reaction. They along with the businessmen in the area liked the design and it was accepted for use.

A design that is finalised should not only strike a balance between the editorial contents (news and features) and the advertising but should also be acceptable to the readers. Vinod Mehta, Editor-in-Chief of Outlook Group of magazines rightly believes that designers have no magic wand. In his Delhi diary in *Outlook* he wrote: "They [designers] need to be exactly guided by an editorial team. If you let designers run riot, they will be probably a publishing disaster. One can construct a beautiful-looking newspaper which is a puzzle for the reader. My own conviction is that the editorial must lead design, and not the other way round". This is what actually happened a few years back when *Outlook* (a weekly magazine from Delhi) changed its design. The type size in the new design was very small and was a strain to the eyes of even young readers. The popular reaction was against the type size. It was so vehement that the Editor had to change the type size along with some other design concepts.

The layout of the newspaper should go with the content of the newspaper for which reliability, dignity and intelligent reporting are essential. The design should be such that a reader can easily find the positioning of various news sections—sports, foreign, political, regional and local. He should know where to look for the news that he wants to read. Every reader is aware that the leading story of the day will occupy the biggest space on page one. But he should also know where to find the sports pages or the editorial opinion, where the city or business section is placed, and where the fashion and film gossip are. The ultimate objective of the newspaper design is to help the reader find the news and features of his choice without wasting time. Therefore, the acquaintance of readers' choices, preferences and habits is the first principle in newspaper design and layout. This is the reason that the layout and design of a newspaper does not change frequently. Whenever it is redesigned, a lot of research goes in about the reading habits and preferences of the readers.

The design of the newspaper should not only indicate where things are located but also the framework in which they appear. Therefore, a fixed typographical format should be given to weather reports and forecasts, and T-20 cricket matches for easy understanding. A distinctive typeface should be used for the headings on the sports page so that it is not mistaken for the news pages. The editorials should appear in a fixed format, set in a special font and column size, and always placed on the same position on the same page every day, probably except Sunday. Distinctive headings or slugs should be given to economic and business news, astrological forecasts, and films and books reviews so that they can be recognised without making much effort. However, it does not mean that there is a stereotype presentation every day. Considerable variation in page pattern is still possible even after allowing for these established styles.

The Objective of Design

After the design of the newspaper has been finalised, daily presentation of news and features becomes an exercise in layout by which the contents are made available to the readers. The daily layout of the newspaper is a process similar to packaging. As is the case with most forms of packaging, the visual display is deep-seated in psychology.

In the past, even 20 years back, there were no design departments in newspaper houses. Sub-editors and news editors used to design the page and prepare it with the help of paste-up artists. They followed no pattern or format. But now because of intense competition, even the local newspapers have become design conscious. Almost every sizeable newspaper, big or small, has a design department headed by a design director. Sometimes he is known as the design editor. He heads the art desk also. This is common with magazines too. The design department prepares the layout of each page in the broad format as decided by the editor. Fonts, illustrations, graphics and pictures are decided and edited by the journalists for each page. The design director supervises the layout of all editorial contents, once the design of the pages has been laid down and the main items placed by the night-editor or chief-sub editor.

Broadly speaking, page designing has three objectives:

Firstly to attract the attention of the reader; *secondly*, to guide him to different stories on the page and indicate their relative

Layout and Design

importance; and *thirdly*, to give a distinct identity to the newspaper and a visual character to each page.

The role of the designer is to use headlines, text and pictures in such a way that a balance is maintained on the page to attract the attention of the reader. When the reader turns the page, the various type sizes should denote the relative importance of each story. Special fonts should help him to recognise regular features. Overall, the balanced and repeated use of certain fonts would give the newspaper a distinct visual character. The paper would be instantly recognisable by the reader as it would look different from the other newspapers.

The strategy for designing a page is to place the various stories in relation to each other so that the readers' eyes are guided to move through the page to look over different stories. The focal point on a page should be the headline and the leading picture. The headlines should be positioned in relation to advertising contents in such a way that a boldly displayed advertisement does not damage the design of the news story. The location of the heading and pictures, thus, perform not only an editorial function but also a design function by being a part of a deliberate composition. Without the relief provided by pictures and variation in fonts, the design would look a grey column mass as in the 18th century papers before design came to matter.

The way the editorial material is used differs from newspaper to newspaper. However, the basic objective of a design, as stated above, remains the same. For example *The Hindu* has a more word-oriented presentation than *The Times of India*. The latter has shorter items and bolder headings and more pictures, producing what is known as the poster technique. The Sunday editions of most of the national dailies have introduced imaginative and creative ways the use of typography, rules and borders, particularly on the features pages. In order to understand these points fully go through various newspapers in your library. Distinctive variations in the same newspaper from different cities can likewise be found if you examine newspapers from different regions.

It is important to understand that the uncontrolled use of bold types, rules, borders and texts should be avoided. The use of these items must serve a purpose and the page should not become flashy, loud or lifeless. It should also not become a typographical hodgepodge. The reader when going through the page must find it reader-friendly. This is known as providing the reader 'eye comfort.' It can be achieved by balancing the colours and not just mixing them thoughtlessly. In other words, there should not be an overuse of colours. Also colours should not be used in the chromatic sense—using all the tones of the chromatic scale. The balance can be maintained by juxtaposing blacks and greys with white space. The quality of colour (that is characterised by its dominant or complementary character and purity taken together) should be kept in mind. If this aspect of design has not been taught in media school, the desk-editor should have a meeting with the design director to understand the use of colours for a better-looking and reader-friendly page.

Page-planning

The national newspapers usually draw up page layouts in detail on full-size or half-size layout sheets so that precise measurements can be taken and detailed instructions written down. These sheets are printed to show standard column widths.

A newspaper page is divided into a fixed number of columns—usually six to eight in a broadsheet and four to six in a tabloid. These columns establish the standard typesetting width to be used in each paper for headlines and text. Headlines, and occasionally text, can appear across multiples of a column: i.e., double column, across three or four columns or, in the case of important headlines across all the columns.

On rare occasions, the layout designer can take liberty to set headlines and text in an arbitrary way, breaking the general layout pattern of the newspaper. The rare occasion happens when the news is of extraordinary importance like the terrorist attack in Mumbai on 26 November 2008. Tabloids, however, use it more occasionally than broadsheet newspapers. They do so as they are more design-oriented than broadsheets.

From the design point of view, a page consists of four elements: text, headlines, pictures and advertisements.

Text is the main reading material in the story. In brief, it is the body matter or body setting of various stories. It normally is set in a regular column-width and in a standard size font that is comfortable for reading. The font size is increased to give prominence to the first few paragraphs or introduction of a story.

Headlines: Every page of a newspaper carries a number of stories that carry headlines of different sizes and widths. These headlines are in a matching font. The desk-editor may like that a particular story should look different. In that case a different font can be given.

The biggest headline on a page is at the top of the page. It is in most of cases the longest story. If it crosses all the columns of the page it is called a *banner* headline or a *streamer*. Its size and prominence indicate that this is the most important story. This is known as the *lead* story. The streamer might have above it a smaller line of heading containing a separate statement. This is known as a *strap-line*, a second headline that comes first and qualifies the main headline.

The second biggest or second most prominent headline indicates the second most important story. This, in the journalistic parlance, is known as the second lead. All other stories with headlines at the top half of the page are called *tops*. These are usually single columns, but can be double column or more depending on the importance of the story and the available space on the page. The lead story, the second lead and the various tops fill the main area of a page. Stories of least importance are placed in the lower half of the page. These mainly contain one, two or three paragraphs with a short headline. Short stories may not carry a headline. They may just have a small heading of one or two lines in small fonts.

The newspapers publishing industry in the United States and Britain usually uses the term 'tops' because of historical reasons. The term is not in much use in India.

When newspapers began to be published, the concept of design did not exist. In those days all stories started at the top of the page and carried only a single column headline. When these stories ended, the space was filled with small stories. This was known as 'vertical layout.' Then the 'horizontal layout' was introduced and became popular. The latter is the modern newspaper design in which stories with sizeable headlines are allowed to cross the page. It makes it possible to place several stories at the bottom half. It was the time when the use of the term 'tops' began to indicate a difference in the stories appearing in the two halves of the page.

Pictures on the page are used to illustrate stories and give a lift to the page. The purpose is to give a visual balance to the page. The size of the picture depends on the size of the story. But many a time a big picture is used with a small story where strong visual impact of the situation needs to be created.

Advertisements form an important section of the page over which the editorial has virtually no control. In fact, the number of pages that the newspaper would have on a particular day depends on the volume of ads. The more the ads the more would be the pages in the newspaper.

Advertisements are collected and scheduled by the advertisement department that works under the direct control of the management. By the afternoon of each day, the advertisement department provides an advertisement dummy to the editorial. It shows spaces allotted to advertisements on each page. This is known as an 'ad dummy,' and indicates the shape and placement of ads on each page of the newspaper. The shape and design of the advertisements is decided between the advertiser and the advertisement department which allots the appropriate space. While preparing an ad dummy efforts are made to balance the pattern of products. This is achieved by avoiding excessive similarity of product on each page. For example, all the ads of soap are not to be given on the same page unless there is a supplement on soaps. In some, the advertisement department guarantees precise placing on the page to the advertiser.

The editorial layout has to follow the ad dummy. The font and contents of an advertisement cannot be altered by the desk-editor. The advertising position is to be changed only if there is a serious clash with editorial content. Also if an important story needs a special placing the advertisements may be shifted or even cancelled. This, however, is to be done in consultation with and the approval of the advertisement manager.

A good newspaper should make it mandatory for the desk-editor to show the advertisement artwork to the design director before he begins to place editorial material on the page. It is to avoid conspicuous clash between the advertisement and the editorial text if the font or picture in the two clash. For example, it would look conflicting if a picture being used in the editorial material is similar to the picture in the advertisement. Similarly, it would create a bad impact if the picture of a collapsed building were shown along with an advertisement of a cement or steel company. Also, it would be not be wise to use a similar font in the story or its heading if it is being used in the advertising slogan on the same page.

Fonts or Typography

Every newspaper has to have a character. It is achieved by the consistent use of a limited number of fonts. One main choice has to be for the news pages and another for the features pages. There should be a regular variant in use in each case. However, fonts must be selected keeping in mind that the desk-editor should be able to handle them under pressures of deadline. The font should also be able to achieve a variety of effects. Large and bold fonts are needed for those special occasions when a really big story demands flashy treatment; more modest typefaces are needed for the general run of reports.

Much has been written and discussed about the philosophy of fonts that newspapers should use. We need not go into details here as a desk-editor is required to have only a functional and elementary knowledge of fonts.

Newspapers take their own decisions on fonts to be used in the publication after consulting the editor. However, editors usually choose from the traditional fonts. Widely circulated newspapers, and those that have been in publication for a long time like *The Times of India*, prefer and have been using the older serif family. Popular tabloids and those broadsheets that want to give a modern look to their newspapers prefer sans serif, which are of recent origin.

Serif and sans serif are two basic families of fonts by which Western alphabets are accomplished. These two are the original typefaces from which hundreds of fonts have come out. Many of them are in use in printing in the contemporary newspaper industry.

Serif font: Serif means short lines stemming from and at an angle to the upper and lower ends of the strokes of a letter. It is the font in which the letters have a serif characteristic—cross-line finishing off each stroke—in the form of a decoration. Times Roman and now Times New Roman is the most popular font that is used by most of the quality newspapers. The specimen of the Times New Roman is given below:

Times New Roman
ABCDEFGHIJKLMNOPQRSTUVWXYZ
1234567890
abcdefghijklmnopqrstuvwxyz
(Times News Roman is very popular in the print media.)

The serif characteristic dates back to the carved Latin inscription of the Romans. The printing presses in the beginning used only black letter text that developed from monastic manuscripts. As the printing technology developed, serif typefaces replaced black letter. However, black letter continued to be the standard for many years in certain parts of Europe. Later, 18th century onwards many distinguished designers evolved different versions of the original Roman seriffed fonts. These fonts are known after the designers names. A few names of these designers are Sir William Caslon (1692–1766), John Baskerville

(1706–1775), Giambattista Bodoni (1740–1813), and Firmin Didot (1764–1836). Its development continued into the 20th century with Stanley Morison's (1899–1967) Times New Roman and others.

Sans serif font: This type is that family of fonts in which there is no serif or decorative cross-line on the strokes of its letters. This font was considered unattractive in the beginning. However, Eric Gill (1882–1940) and other imaginative designers of the 20th century made this font popular as this family was considered bold and elegant. As its use increased. a varied range of sans serif fonts developed. Arial and Courier New are the two widely used sans fonts. The specimens of both these fonts are given below:

Arial
ABCDEFGHIJKLMNOPQRSTUVWXYZ
1234567890
abcdefghijklmnopqrstuvwxyz

Courier New
ABCDEFGHIJKLMNOPQRSTUVWXYZ
1234567890
abcdefghijklmnopqrstuvwxyz

Use of Fonts

Serif and sans serif are used widely in various forms. Both have their admirers and critics. Serif font is still popular as it provides for comfortable reading. Generation after generation during the past four centuries has been reading newspapers printed using this font. It is more readable even in a small size because it is less uniform than sans. Reading comfort is the main reason why it continues to be used in setting the body text in newspapers. Even those newspapers that use sans, use serif font for headings. Most of the standard books throughout the world use the various ranges of serif for setting their text. Its several modern designs have become popular in advertising typography. Special versions such as Playbill and Rockwell Condensed dominate theatre poster advertising. The larger serif ranges such as Placard and the various forms of Gothic Titling give great boldness to headlines in tabloid newspapers. Some elegant sans serif ranges such as Record Gothic and the various condensed Gothics make useful variants in papers that have chosen a predominantly serif format.

Over time the two font families have grown enormously in numbers. Each font family has further developed into condensed and expanded versions, and also into old italic versions, as well as the standard or roman. The bold has a flatter stroke and the italic a sloping configuration. There is also sometimes a light version in which the stroke is thinner than the standard or roman. In all these variants, the dominant design characteristic is maintained. Thus, in a popular serif face such as Century, which is used by many newspapers as its standard news type, the expanded, or wider version is still Century, as is the light and the italic versions.

It is, therefore, possible for newspapers to use a type such as Century and achieve a varied and attractive format without departing from the type characteristic of the Century type format. This can be achieved by using the expanded, light and italic versions.

Several other variations are also possible. These can be obtained within a fixed font by having some headlines in capital letters (caps), and others in small or lowercase (lc). Some newspapers prefer homogeneity and this can be accomplished by giving all headlines in lower case versions, in bold, light or italic, of a particular font. Such rigidity tends to be limited to page-one and the inside news pages. For the features pages more variety of fonts is available, with the choice of a variant, rarely extending into an entirely different or opposed typeface.

Some newspapers use lighter and more decorative fonts for special contents such as the children's pages or sports pages, and an entirely alien bold font might be introduced to project a special serialisation.

Layout and Design

Many a time tabloids use Condensed Sans, a predominantly serif format face, for a special item in the middle of a news page (called kicker in the American parlance). It requires the text to be set in a bold body type. Sometimes tabloids also set a headline in Ludlow Black (a serif type with very fat serif) in the sans serif format on its news page. Whatever method is adopted, correct use of white space between the words in headlines and text and also between the lines is important. It is to project balance while using different types of fonts.

Whatever variations are introduced and for whatever purpose, the newspaper for its page design should decide upon one standard font for all important pages. It should be used consistently. This is the only way the newspaper can achieve its design character and font standardisation. An analysis of successive editions of any newspaper—national, regional, or local—will prove this point. A total change of font is rarely done by Indian newspapers, and is usually coupled with a re-launch or a merger with another paper.

Font Measurement

The measurement in the printing industry is not in inches or centimetres but in a 275-year-old system of points. Seventy-two (72) points make an inch. Defined in this way, an 18-point letter would be one-fourth of an inch depth; a 36-point letter would be half an inch deep and so on. In fact, it should be remembered that this measurement was thought of when the fonts were mounted on the metal base. In earlier days of printing the shape of the letter was fixed on a metal base. The point size was the measurement of the metal base upon which the shape of the letter rose. The typesetting is no more metal based (it is online on computers), but the old pattern of point measurement is still followed (as the upper case and the lower case for capitals and small letters respectively). Another point to remember is that with lower case letters some, like a 'k', have ascenders that stick above. Others, like 'g', have descenders that hang below. Some like an 'f' and a 'j' have both ascenders and descenders that are accommodated on the metal base of the type in its traditional form.

The size of the font, therefore, is the height from the bottom of the descender to the top of the ascender. The constant depth of the letter, assuming there is neither ascender nor descender, is called the 'x' height. This can vary according to whether or not the particular typeface is designed with long ascenders and descenders. As a result a 36-point line with a big 'x' height looks bigger than a 36-point line with a small 'x' height. It should be clear that though an inch has 72 points, the actual measurable depth of the type that prints is always less than that, and can vary in its 'x' height from font to font, depending on the design.

It is always better not to remember the relation between an inch and points. The reason is that fonts are used in a series of standard point sizes that desk editors quickly learn to use and recognise. These sizes ascend in a regular order starting with the smallest body type and rising to a normal maximum of 144 points. Higher point fonts are mostly used only in popular tabloids. Broadsheets use them only on rare occasions to report unprecedented news like onset of a war, a terrorist attack as in Mumbai on 26 November 2008, the September 11 air attack on New York, or man landing on the moon.

Typefaces used	
Used in Text:	5 ½, 6, 7, 8, 9, 10, 12, 14
Used in headlines:	14, 18, 24, 30, 36, 42, 48, 60, 72, 84, 96, 120, 144

The smaller size fonts are rarely referred to in a few newspaper offices by their old names which are:

5½ pt	ruby
2 pt	nonpareil (pronounced nonprul)
7 pt	minion (usually min)
8 pt	brevier (breveer or brev)
9 pt	bourgeois (burjoyce or bjs)
10 pt	long primer (primer or LP)
12 pt	pica

Normally small body size fonts are available only in a limited number and they seldom exceed 14 points. A newspaper will adopt one of these as its text material for reading and will vary it only occasionally. In headline sizes great many faces are available from 14 points upwards. These are available from both the serif and the sans serif families. The newspapers use one or two such faces only in headlines. However, the desk-editors are given the liberty to use their variants to create a better impact.

A good newspaper should develop a font booklet to list a selection of each font in its available sizes, in caps and lower cases. It helps in making a count of the number of letters needed for each line of headline according to the font chosen. The font booklet should show the specimens in standard column widths and multiples of columns. This information is useful for desk-editors who have to write headlines within the scheduled time. Most of the time they are working against the clock and so readymade information is advantageous.

It is important for desk-editors to understand 'point measurement' because it gives an idea of the size of the font. It helps them to determine the number of letters that can be accommodated in a headline of a given width. However, there is another form of measurement that desk-editors need to know about. It is known as font measure and is used for the width of the type setting.

Font measure is calculated in 'em' and 'en', or what are referred to by printers as 'muttons' and 'nuts.' An 'em' is the width of a standard 12-point roman letter 'm', which, in fact is 12 points wide as well as deep. Since an 'em' equals 12 points, six 'em' is equal to an inch. An 'en' is equal to a standard 12-point roman letter 'n', and is half the size of an 'em'. Therefore, 12 'en' are equal to an inch.

In the newspaper jargon when one refers to pica it means 'em' or 12 points. Therefore, when mentioning a standard column width of newspapers it is said that a broadsheet has a 9½-em or an 11-em column, which would always mean pica em. In fact, in normal usage em is referred to as pica. It is the practice in sub-editing to mention 'single column,' 'double column,' 'across three columns,' to mention the space to be given to a story.

If the keyboard system is being used for type setting the desk-editor, when using the non-standard measure, should mark up the accurate measure in em. It is necessary and important because despite the flexibility of the photo-typesetting system the traditional measurements of type-size and setting-widths are used.

Picture Editing

The final aspect of page layout and design is picture editing. Like page design, picture design is more aesthetic, imaginative and creative and less technical. However, technical aspect of picture editing is important because without it photo editing cannot be imaginative and creative. In fact, imagination, and a good deal of experience, is required to select a photograph from a bunch and decide that it will be the right picture that will print well and enhance the page.

The most important factor in picture editing is to find out how relevant the picture is to the story. Next is to see how the picture would be positioned in the space available for it in the story. For example, when set in the story, the figures in the picture should not look out of the page or away from the story that the photograph illustrates. In certain cases, in 'head' shots for instance, it may be necessary to reverse the print for better effects. By reversing the face the eyes would look in the required direction. This, however, should not harm the image in any way or make nonsense of background detail.

Also important are the picture's general composition and its tonal qualities. A photograph of predominantly grey tones will not print well on newsprint that is not good for fine details.

A photograph has to be selected from a bunch of relevant pictures. These may be related with a particular person or an incident. The process of rejecting and short-listing is to be adopted. The desk-editor has to select a few pictures for the final choosing. The final selection can be done by the desk-editor in charge of the page or the chief sub-editor or the news editor. It all depends on the importance of the story and the page. All page-one pictures are to be approved by the editor when in office. In his absence, the designated person takes this decision and makes the final choice. The desk-editor in charge of the page normally decides photographs for all other pages. Nevertheless, the chief sub-editor and news editor have the right to change the picture. The advice of the photo editor is also sought when dealing with important stories. Once the photograph has been chosen and its position on the page decided, its actual editing is to be done by the artist.

Picture editing is not usually done by the chief photographer. The job of the chief photographer is only to brief photographers, gather and provide pictures and run the picture desk. In small newspapers, generally local, there is not much specialisation. The newspaper has only a few pages and is brought out by a very small number of persons. In such newspapers normally the editor decides on the pictures.

The next aspect of picture editing is to decide how much and what part of the picture is to be used with the story. In other words a decision has to be taken on what parts of the picture are not relevant for the story. These are the persons or details not essential to the story. In certain cases, certain persons may have to be excluded from the picture because of legal reasons. This aspect of picture editing is known as *cropping*, which means to alter the size and shape of the photograph. This job is done by the artist on the computer. Earlier it was done manually.

The picture before being used in the newspaper is to be retouched. The amount of retouching to be done depends on the quality of the original picture. A picture that is important for the story but is of poor quality would need heavy retouching. However, nothing should be added to a picture because it may be legally dangerous.

Retouching of the picture is done by an artist who is known as the *retoucher*. However, the editor is wholly responsible for the cropped and retouched picture (as he is responsible for every printed word in the newspaper) when the picture gets printed in the newspaper. Any legal liability for misrepresentation or even libel (for example, for changing the features of a person) arising out of the retouching carried out by the art department is of the editor and not of the artist who retouched it. A newspaper, therefore, should scrutinise all final prints of pictures editorially for this purpose.

Every newspaper whether using the old traditional method or the modern computerised system should follow the same layout and design basics. The type has to be chosen to give balance and a consistent overall character. Pictures are to be cropped and scaled in the same way. The body text, headlines, illustrations and graphics, and advertisements have to be placed in relation to each other to achieve an attractive design, whether the pages are made up in the metal, pieced together with scissors and paste, or assembled on a screen.

Glossary

ABC Audit Bureau of Circulation, the organisation that provides independent confirmation of the circulation by way of sales of a newspaper or magazine.

In India the Audit Bureau of Circulations (ABC) was founded in 1948 as a non-profit, voluntary organisation. It consists of publishers, advertisers and advertising agencies. ABC is a founder member of the International Federation of Audit Bureaux of Circulations.

The main function of ABC is to evolve and lay down a standard and uniform procedure by which a member publisher computes its net paid sales. The circulation figures have to be checked, verified and certified by a Chartered Accountant (CA) who is to be selected from the panel that is approved by the ABC. The certificate has to be issued every six months stating that the figures have been verified according to the rules and regulations set by the ABC.

ABC has a membership of 411 publishers of newspapers and magazines, 151 advertising agencies, 51 advertisers and 20 news agencies and associations connected with print media and advertising. ABC-certified figures are an important factor for advertisers for choosing advertising media, as an Advertiser would like to know the reach before advertising. The ABC figures are not based on opinions, claims or guesswork. They are prepared on the basis of rigid, in-depth and impartial audits of paid circulation by independent and leading CAs.

Ad dummy	Miniature grid of the newspaper on which the size and placement of advertisements are marked.
Ad:ed ratio	The ratio of advertising to editorial in a newspaper or magazine. In India the newspapers have to maintain an ad:ed ratio prescribed by law.
Ad rule	The rule that separates advertisements from the editorial matter.
Ad-feature	An editorial feature commissioned not by the editor but by the advertisement department. The objective is to encourage advertising with the help of editorial material that the editorial can help in preparing. The articles and ads go side by side.
Advertorial	An article prepared with the material provided by those who give an advertisement. It is written and designed by the advertising client to promote its objective or product. It should not look similar to the editorial material. But nowadays many newspapers are not following this rule and present the advertorial the same way the editorial material is being presented.
All rights	The newspaper purchases the copyright from the contributor to publish his piece as many times as it wants and in any territory without any further payment. The contributor cannot use it again without the written permission of the newspaper.
Angle	The newspaper adopting a particular point of interest in a news story. The story is written to promote that view throughout.
Appraisal	A meeting of the editor with the HR head to assess the annual performance of journalists for the annual raise.
Artwork	The physical components of a page or an advertisement, including half tones and typesetting, before it is converted into film.
Ascender	The upper strokes of lower case letters as b, d, h, etc.
Assign	The contributor selling all his rights to the newspaper.
Attribution	It is the direction to get a quote or information from the source. A note 'quote' in a copy is made to suggest that a quotation of the person who talked to the reporter or spoke publicly be given.
Background	The context in which a story, article or feature is being written. It also means a brief historical backdrop so that readers can understand the story better.

Glossary

Back issue	A previous copy of the newspaper or magazine.
Backup	Another copy of the story or article to be kept for use if the originals are lost or damaged. Backup can be stored in a CD or pen drive. The hard copy is also one form of backup.
Bad-break	It means repulsive or misleading results because of automatic hyphenation, e.g. 'therapists' becoming 'the rapist'.
Barcode	A machine-readable serial number placed on a magazine cover.
Baseline	An imaginary line along the bottom of a row of type. Descenders fall below the baseline.
Bleed	To extend the print area beyond the boundary of the page. This is to give additional prominence to the matter being printed. Pictures are many a times printed to 'bleed'. Text is seldom printed in bleed.
Blob par	A black dot or bullet at the beginning of a paragraph. It is used to highlight extra points of interest.
Body copy or body text	The main text of a story or article or feature.
Body type	The font that is to be used in setting the body of the story.
Bold	The same word with heavy type so that it becomes prominent.
Boost	A box that suggests to the reader what would be in the story or the article in the next edition or issue. This is to ensure that the reader does not miss the next part.
Box	Additional or important material given in an area marked out by rules all around. This normally provides more information or background to the central point mentioned in the story.
Brainstorming Session	A meeting in which participants think widely and give even wild suggestions without giving critical comments.
Brief	It means instructions to a reporter, correspondent, writer, photographer or designer by the editor or chief of bureau or chief reporter before beginning the assignment. Sometimes it may also mean a short news item.

Bromide	Photographic paper produced by a typesetting or image-setting machine.
Browser	Computer programs used for reading the world wide web pages.
Bug	An electronic pick-up for secretly listening and recording conversations on telephone between two persons.
Bullet	A black dot used for emphasis.
Business-to-Business	The current term for trade magazines. These are meant only for those in that particular business and are tailored; not meant for the general reader.
Bust	To be too long for the space allocated. Used for headlines, straplines and captions.
By-line	The author's name when used on the page.
Caps	It means that the marked letters are to be set in capital.
Caption	The text given to a picture or a photograph to indicate what it shows
Caret mark	A mark used in copy mark-up and proof-reading to indicate that something must be inserted.
Cast off	To calculate the space occupied by a piece of text.
Catch-line	A short identifying name given to a story as it passes through the production process.
CD-ROM	Compact disc used to display words, images, sound and moving pictures on a computer screen.
Centred	A form of typesetting in which equal space is provided at both ends of each line.
Classified	Small advertisements that are set in a single column and are grouped together to indicate particular interest. For example, all matrimonial classifieds are displayed separately. These are charged per line or per word.
Classified display	Advertisements in the classified columns that are given prominence by rules and use of bold or larger font. An extra charge is made for this service.
Clip art	Pictures not subject to copyright restrictions, usually obtained in digitised form.
Close	To send an edition or issue to the printers. It is indicated by marking: 'The edition/issue is closed.'

Glossary

Colour house	Where photographs are scanned and united with electronically generated pages and type to produce the film required to make printing plates.
Colour separations	The four separate pieces of film created when full-colour material is put through the four-colour process.
Column	It normally means the division of a newspaper or magazine page into vertical lengths. A broadsheet is divided into six or eight columns. Nowadays since the broadsheets have shortened their size many newspapers use seven columns. The tabloids and magazines use three or four columns. It also means a regular article written by the same person every week or fortnight.
Columnist	A person who writes regularly on a particular subject or in a special place in the newspaper or magazine. He expresses his own views on the subject and is not subject to editing.
Column rule	Vertical lines that separate columns.
Commission	A contract asking a freelance writer or photographer to produce a piece of work.
Computer-to-plate	Sending finished pages from the editorial layout system to create a printing plate, with an interim film stage. It is also known as 'straight to plate'.
Contact sheet	A sheet of photographs made by pressing the negatives directly against the photographic paper. The prints are the same size as the original negatives.
Contacts	Persons who provide information to journalists for stories.
Contacts book	The notebook that lists the telephone numbers of contacts of a journalist. This is a highly secretive and valued document.
Contempt of court	Illegal interference with the course of justice.
Copy	Written, typewritten or emailed material which is used for editing.
Copy desk	The place of work where copy editors work and edit copies for final approval. All editorial copies have to pass through the copy desk.
Copy editor	The person who prepares the editorial copy for the page.
Copy-flow	The movement of journalistic material during the editing and production process.

Copyright	Ownership of original material and the material published in newspapers, magazines and books. The right to reproduce a piece of creative work is initially held by its creator. But it can be purchased by others.
Cover	The first page of a magazine. It also means to attend and prepare a report of an activity to be used in the newspaper.
Coverage	The extent of attention that a newspaper gives to a particular activity, happening or event.
Cover-line	Words used on the cover to attract readers.
Cover-mount	A free gift attached to the cover.
Credits	Details of photographers, authors, and journalists that go alongside photographs or published material. Credits to photographs are usually given in small font below or on the side of the picture.
Cromalin	A proprietary proofing system for proofing four-colour material from film rather than printing plates.
Crop	To reduce the size and shape of a photograph either to highlight a particular area or to fit it in the allotted space.
Crosshead	A small headline in the body of the text. It is put between paragraphs.
Cross-reference	A reminder to readers that further information on a subject is to be found elsewhere in an issue.
Cut	To delete a section of text.
Cut-out	Removing all the background from the photograph. The picture appears in silhouette.
Cuttings	Articles, news stories and editorials that have been published earlier. These are kept in files and are used for reference purposes. In the American jargon these are known as clippings. Cuttings are not much in use presently because of the Internet.
Database	Information organised and stored in a computer.
Deadline	The time by which a journalist is expected to complete his assignment.
Deck	In the true sense of the word it is one complete headline, no matter how many lines it occupies. A subheading beneath it in a different font or size would be a second deck. Often used, erroneously to mean a single line of headline type; a two-line headline is thus called a two-deck headline.

Glossary

Delete	To remove a character, word or line from the text.
Departments	An American jargon, now widely used, for the regular elements found in each issue of a magazine like letters, Sports, Economy, Leisure etc.
Descender	The tail of certain lower case letters (p,q,y, etc) which descends below the baseline.
Desk	The department that is responsible for the editing of a newspaper or magazine. Besides the central news desk, there can be specialised editing desks like the features desk, sports desk, and business desk.
Desktop publishing	The computer hardware and software system for typesetting and make-up of pages, complete with photographs, on-screen.
Disk	A computer storage medium, available in fixed 'hard disk' or portable 'CD disk' form.
Display ad	General advertisements in the newspaper that are usually designed by the advertisement agencies. These are supplied in the art work form. These ads use more than simple fonts and appear outside the classified section.
Display Font	Large font used for headlines.
Domain	Fundamental part of the address of a computer within the Internet.
Double-page spread	(DPS) Two pages opposite each other, whether used for single advertisement or a single editorial.
Drop cap	The first letter of the feature, or the paragraph that covers more than one line and hangs below the top line. It is a large letter usually at least as deep as two lines of body type.
Dropout	It indicates a fault in camerawork or plate-making which means that the light areas of a picture will lose all detail.
Dummy	(a) A mock-up of a new publishing or of the existing newspaper for design experiments, rearrangements, launching and promotional uses; (b) in a daily newspaper it is a miniature newspaper on dummy sheets indicating the location of various news items and other features; (c) in a magazine it is the complete set of proofs in correct order; (d) a miniature on paper to show the location of display advertisements.

Dummy run	Producing a new newspaper or section of it up to any stage short of actual publication.
Duotone	A black and white picture reproduced by printing in black and one other colour.
Edit	It is the process of deleting, checking, rewriting and improving news stories, features and articles.
Editorial	(a) The journalistic content of a newspaper or magazine; (b) the leader column that expresses the view of the newspaper or the magazine on some critical issue.
Editor's letter	Introductory remarks by the editor on some important issue. It is published on the first page of the newspaper and contains his signature.
Electronic mail (email)	A means of communicating by typing messages into a computer. It is transmitted through the Internet.
Em	(a) A unit of measurement that was used for a long time but now is becoming archaic. An em, properly called a pica, is 12 points. It represents the space occupied by an upper case M in 12-pt font. (b) Historically, an em in any type size is the width of an upper case M in that size. Thus, a 9-pt em is 9pts wide; an 8-pt is 8 pts and so on.
Ends	It is written at the end of a piece of original copy to indicate that there is no more material to add and the article or the story is finished. It is to ensure that the desk received the full manuscript.
End symbol	A typographic device (usually a black square or bullet) used in magazine pages to indicate that the story or the article has finished.
Exclusive	A story or interview that is published only in a particular newspaper or magazine.
Facing matter	An advertisement that is placed opposite the editorial.
Fair comment	A defence to certain libel actions.
Feature	A piece of writing that is longer, more descriptive and contains more 'colour' than a news story.
Fifth colour	The use of an extra colour to create a striking effect beyond the means of the normal four-colour process. It is mainly used on covers of the magazine.
File	A document created on computer.
File name	The name that is given to a computer document.

Glossary

Fill	When a story does not fit in the allotted space it is rewritten to fit in the given space. It can be a story, article, feature, headline, strapline or introduction.
Film	Material produced by image-setting machines and colour-separation equipment and used to make printing plates.
First right	The right of the newspaper to publish an article once. It cannot be published in any other newspaper or magazine before that. But once it is published, the writer is free to use it in other publications.
Fit	To enlarge or shorten a piece of writing to fit in the allotted space.
Flash	A design device to attract attention.
Focus	Concentration on the identity of a newspaper or magazine.
Focus group	A group of readers and potential readers assembled for research purposes.
Folio	Page number.
Follow-up	A return to a story later to provide new developments and reactions.
Footer	A line, often including the magazine's name that appears at the bottom of every page.
Format	(a) The size and shape of a page, e.g. broadsheet, tabloid or A-4; (b) all the typographic specifications that are laid down in a magazine's design. Nowadays formatting is done automatically when the text is transferred into a layout programme.
Fount or font	Traditionally, a set of character in one typeface and one size. Today, it tends to mean a typeface in its complete range and italic and bold varieties.
Four-colour process	It is a printing technique that uses four colours of ink (cyan, magenta, yellow and black) to simulate full colour.
Freelancer	A journalist who does not work as a regular employee; either works writing at home or working as a casual sub-editor.
Furniture	(a) Design elements common to every page of a newspaper or magazine; (b) regular features and fixed items in the magazine as a whole. The term is commonly used in the U.K. and the U.S.A.; not popular in India

Galley proof	A proof produced as a single column of type, before page make-up. Now it is no more in use because of the use of modern electronic techniques.
Gatefold	A page, usually the inside front cover, which folds in or out to accommodate a large advertisement.
Gone to bed	The newspaper or magazine is closed for the edition and is sent to the printers. After this nothing can be changed.
Graduated tint	A tint that changes in density or hue from top to bottom or from side to side.
Grid	The underlying design structure of the newspaper or magazine, determining column widths and image areas. Now usually exists only in computer form.
Gutter	The gap between two columns or two adjoining pages.
Half-tone	An illustration or photograph after it has been broken into dots for printing.
Hard copy	The computer copy on paper and not on the computer screen.
Header	A line of type that appears at the top of every page.
Heading or headline	Title given to a story, feature or article. It is an area of display type that draws the reader's interest to a story or feature.
Hold over	That material that cannot be used in the current edition or magazine. It is to be kept for the next edition or issue or some future date.
Hot links	Words or graphics on a page of computer text that can be clicked to take the reader to a different page.
House ad	An advertisement placed in a newspaper or magazine by its own publisher.
House journal	A magazine produced for the employees of an organisation.
House style	A set of rules about disputed spellings, matters of punctuation, capitalisation, use of numbers and similar things.
HTML	HyperText Mark-up Language is a computer language used for the creation of World Wide Web pages.
Human interest	A type of story or feature that is written to show the emotional aspects of human lives.

Glossary

HyperText	Text on a computer screen that can be clicked on to allow the reader to navigate around a page, document, or site.
Hyphenation	The insertion of a hyphen into a word as it breaks at the end of a line. It is an automatic process as it is controlled by dictionaries built into the desktop publishing programs. However, it can be manually overriden in case the desk-editor finds the hyphenation absurd.
Icon	A drawing on a computer screen used to indicate and manipulate files, discs, and drives and so on. It also includes similar drawings used for illustrations and graphics in page design.
Image area	The part of a page that is normally printed.
Imprint	The names and addresses of the publisher and printer and any other legally required information.
Indentation	A shorter line than usual, leaving white spaces at the beginning or end. It is used to markup paragraphs and is abbreviated to 'indent', which is commonly used in place of the full word.
Injunction	A court order to prohibit certain action or actions.
Insert	A loose advertisement or announcement that is placed in the inside pages of the newspaper or magazine.
Internet	The international network of linked computers.
Intro	The opening paragraph given by the editor or desk or sub-editor to a news story or feature and to an article by the author. It is the abbreviation of 'introduction'. It should not be confused with a strapline that is given by an editor, a desk editor or a sub-editor.
Italic	Sloping type used for emphasis, book or title.
Justification	Adjustment of the spacing between words and characters. Justified type is set so that the lines are full out at both ends, and for proving the truth of an allegation when defending a libel action.
Kern	To reduce space between two letters to make them fit neatly. Computer systems do this automatically, but it can be adjusted manually also.
Kicker	An introductory heading in small type above the main heading. The term is used in the United States and not in India.

Kill	To drop a story or feature and not use it later either.
Kill fee	The payment that has to be made for not using a story that has been dropped but was commissioned.
Landscape	A picture or photograph with a horizontal emphasis.
Layout	Design for pages, spreads and features; and the printed versions of those designs.
Lead	The most important and prominent story on a news page. It is pronounced as 'leed'.
Leading	The vertical space between the lines of type. It is measured in points and is pronounced as 'leeding'.
Legal	A potential legal problem or query. A sentence often said in the news room is, "We have got a legal on this page".
Letter spacing	Adjustment of the space between a group of letters to improve appearance. Also known as 'tracking'.
Libel	A defamatory publication or statement.
Lift	To acquire writings or pictures from some other published source without paying for them.
Line drawing	An illustration that uses lines rather than areas of continuous tone.
Listings	Details of events, entertainment etc.
Literal	A typographical error.
Logo	Abbreviation for 'logotype' that means the magazine's name in the typographical style used on the cover.
Lowercase	Small letters, as opposed to capitals.
Manuscript	Original copy on paper.
Mark up	To prepare typewritten copy for typesetting.
Masthead	The panel that includes the name, address, and telephone numbers and often the staff box of a newspaper or magazine. Sometimes it is used to indicate only the title of the newspaper or magazine. But that is incorrect.
Measure	The width of a column. Often measured in pica ems.
Media pack	Details of a newspaper or magazine's circulation, readership and technical specifications. Practiced to attract advertisements.
mf	Abbreviation for 'more follows'. It is written at the end of each page of the copy.

Glossary

Mono	Black and white.
Mug-shot	Simple identifying picture of an individual person.
Multimedia	Bringing together words, images, sounds and moving pictures to be accessed on a computer.
Newsgroup	An Internet discussion group that usually discusses gossip having little real news element.
Newsletter	A magazine with minimal production values distributed for information only.
Next week/month box	A box or panel that indicates the contents in the next issue of the magazine.
nib	Used for a one-paragraph story, Abbreviation for 'news in brief'.
Offline	An electronic medium that does not require a connection to a remote control.
Off the record	A statement made subject to restrictions as to how it is reported.
Online	An electronic medium that requires a connection to a remote computer.
Online service	A commercial organisaton selling information to those connecting to its remote computers.
On spec	A feature offered for the editor's perusal, without obligation.
On the record	A statement made without restrictions as to how it is to be reported.
Orphan	A short line at the beginning and the end of a paragraph appearing at the bottom of the column.
Outs	Photographs submitted for a layout but not used.
Overmatter	Material in excess of the space allowed for it.
Ozalid	A type of proof.
Page rate	The price that a page of advertising can fetch on a page of editorial or the sum that an editor can spend on such a page.
Page traffic	Measurement of how well a given page is read.
Pagination	The number of pages in a magazine.
Panel	An area of type enclosed by rules and often backed by a tint.
Pantone	A property colour-matching system. Fifth colours are sometimes called 'Pantone colours' because this is the system used to define them.

Par/para	Short form for paragraph.
Paste up	To create pages from bromides of type and half-tones, ready to go before the camera. Effectively replaced by desktop publishing programs.
pdf	A computer file in Adobe's portable document format, commonly used for the final output of editorial pages.
Peg	The event to which a story or feature has to be tied to make it topical for example: "The peg for this story is the role of Raj Kumar in the Aarushi murder case".
Perfect bound	A method of binding, using glue that creates a magazine with a hard, square spine.
Photomontage	A photograph assembled out of several originals or extensively retouched.
Pica	12-pt type. A pica em is a 12-pt em. The pica em is used as a unit of typographical measurement.
Picture by-line	A by-line incorporating a photograph of the author.
Pixillate	To treat a picture electronically so that the subject is unrecognisable. Used to protect anonymity in stories where this is legally necessary, and in imitation of television practices
Plaintiff	A person or organisation bringing a legal action, now officially called a 'claimant'.
Planning meeting	A meeting dedicated to future issues.
Plate	An ink-bearing surface used in the lithographic printing process.
Point	The fundamental unit of typographical measurement. There are 72 pts to an inch and 28.35 to a centimetre.
Portfolio	It means either (a) group of magazines owned by a single company; or (b) a folder showing examples of a designer's work.
Portrait	A picture with vertical emphasis.
Post-mortem	A meeting to discuss the previous edition or issue.
Preface	The introductory material to a story or feature, written by the desk editor or sub-editor to explain the purpose, perspective and the scope of the feature or article.
Pre-plan	A meeting to discuss future stories or features.
Pre-press	Print planning, film assembly, plate-making and other activities required before printing.

Glossary

Preprint	A section of a newspaper edition or magazine printed in advance and then inserted into the edition or issue.
Print run	The total number of copies of a newspaper or magazine to be printed.
Prior restraint	Legal action preventing publication.
Privilege	A defence to some liable actions.
Profile	A portrait in words, usually of a person but occasionally of an organisation, a place or an object.
Proof	A printed copy of work-in-progress for checking purposes.
Pull quote	A quote extracted from a feature or news story and given visual emphasis by typography.
Ragged right	Type that is not justified, but is 'flush left' or ranged left. Each line may be a different length, giving a 'ragged' appearance.
Ranged left	Type that is not justified but is lined up on the left.
Ranged right	Type that is not justified but is lined up on the right.
Readership	The total number of people reading a newspaper or magazine. Based on research into how many people see each copy.
Register	The correct alignment of all four colours of ink. Printing can be 'in register' or 'out of register'.
Regulars	The repeated elements in a newspaper or magazine—contents page, editor's letter, news, letters etc.
Reportage	Term used for 'gritty' investigative news features, with appropriate photography.
Repro	Abbreviation for 'reproduction', meaning high level scanning of colour pictures and their reuniting with type and page layouts to make four-colour films required for colour printing.
Repro house	Also known as 'colour house'; facility specialising in reproduction and colour work.
Retouch	To improve or alter a photograph; done electronically nowadays.
Revenue	Income.
Reverse out	It means to show the white type emerging from the black background; sometimes known as a 'wob'—'white on black'.
Right of reply	Procedure for correcting published errors.

Ring-round	News story or feature based on telephone calls seeking instant reactions to events.
River	White space on a page that forms an ugly river-like pattern through a column.
Roman	The standard upright style of type.
Rough	A designer's sketch leading to a finished layout or giving guidance to a photographer.
Rule	Any line appearing in the printed matter.
Runaround	Type that is set to run around a photograph or a graphic element.
Running turn	Ensuring that sentences carry on from one column to the next and from one page to the next. This is to ensure that the reader does not leave the story or feature without reading further.
Saddle-stitching	A method of binding magazines. It is done by folding pages at the seam and stapling them.
Scanner	An electronic or computer device used for converting photographs, artwork and typewritten copy into the digital form.
Scanning	The process of converting photographs, artwork and typewritten copy into digital form.
Scitex	Equipment that is used at the colour house for the manipulation and enhancement of colour photographs at high resolution.
Screamer	An exclamation mark.
Search engine	A program on a Website used for finding things on the Internet.
Section	A part of the magazine formed from a single sheet of paper before being stitched and trimmed.
Server	A computer used for storing large volumes of material, either in the office or as part of the Internet.
Shoot	A photographic section.
Sidebar	Additional material enhancing a story or feature often used in a panel or box to one of the body copy.
Sidehead	A small heading in the text, flush with the left of the columns of type.
Slander	Spoken defamation.
Slug	A small heading at the top of a page to define the nature of the material present on the page below—'News', 'National', 'City', 'International', 'Sports' etc.

Glossary

Solus ad	The only advertisement on a spread.
Solus reader	A reader who is loyal to a single newspaper or magazine.
Special feature	An ad-get feature. It is an editorial feature commissioned by the advertisement department and not the editor to encourage advertising to take space alongside.
Spike	A metal spike for filing which is used for holding any discarded copy. A story that is filed but is not used in the newspaper is 'spiked.' In the present times it is not used as it has been banned for safety reasons. However, it is still used for a similarly named area in a computer system for rejected copies.
Splash	The front-page lead story in a newspaper or in a newspaper-formatted magazine.
Sponsorship	Selling one or more advertisers the right to associate themselves with some editorial area or event. The purpose is to generate more revenue.
Spot colour	Single colour in addition to black.
Spread	A double-page spread.
s/s	Abbreviation for 'same-size'.
Standing artwork	The graphic material that is used in every issue or edition.
Standing matter	The written text that is used in every issue or edition.
Stet	Latin for 'it stands'. It is an instruction to reinstate something shown as deleted on the hard copy or proof.
Sting	The central and the most damaging allegation in a libel case.
Strap or strapline	An additional heading above or below the main heading. It is normally given in small letters.
Strict liability	A type of contempt of court that can be committed accidentlly.
Style book	The repository of house style.
Style sheet	It may either mean (a) a shorter version of a style book; or (b) in desktop publishing programs a stored set of type specifications to which incoming text can be made to conform.
Stylist	The person responsible for organising a photographic shoot, especially if models are involved.

Sub	A sub-editor; also known as a copy editor.
Subhead	A subsidiary heading that usually is given below the main heading in small type.
SWOT	It is a widely practiced exercise to indicate the strengths, weaknesses, opportunities and threats to analyse the position of newspapers or magazines in the market.
Synopsis	A brief summary of an article.
Teeline	A shortened system favoured by journalists.
Thick piece	A ruminative feature.
Thumbnail	A miniature print-out or drawing of a page.
TIFF	Abbreviation of 'Tagged Image File Format'. It is used for a format for storing images in digital form.
Tint	A printed area covered in the typographical form used on the cover.
TOT	Abbreviation for 'Triumph Over Tragedy'. It is used for an emotional story built on human suffering but with a happy ending.
Transparency	A single frame of positive photographic film.
Transpose	To reorder characters, words or paragraphs.
Trim lines	Lines indicating the printing area in desktop publishing software.
Turn arrow	A symbol at the end of a typed page telling the reader to turn the page.
Typeface	A complete alphabet in a particular design.
Typo	Abbreviation for 'typographical error.'
Unfair dismissal	Any dismissal that is not in accordance with the employment law.
Unjustified	Type that has not been made flush at both ends of a line.
Upper-and-lower	A headline regime in which upper case and lower case letters are used, as opposed to 'all-capitals' or 'initial capitals'.
Variable direct costs	Costs that increase as the print run and pagination increase.
Variance	A situation in which the actual expenditure is different than the budgeted one.
Vignette	A photograph that fades away to nothing at the edges.

Glossary

Virus	A computer program designed to spread and damage either hardware or software.
Vox pop	A feature or story based on short interviews and mug shots of members of the public.
Web browser	A computer program for reading the World Wide Web pages.
Web editing	A computer program used to create Web pages.
Web editor	A computer programmer who creates or edits web pages.
Weblog	An individual or group diary published as a Web page, using software designed to create easily updated pages.
Web pages	An individual document in World Wide Web format. It includes words, photographs and graphics.
Website	A group of related World Wide pages.
White space	Unprinted area used by a designer to direct the eye. It also gives relief to the reader against a heavy page that contains too much reading material in black.
Widow	The last line of a paragraph appearing at the top of a column. It should be avoided as far as possible.